Consumer Insights. Findings from Behavioral Research

Consumer Insights: Findings from Behavioral Research

MSI Relevant Knowledge Series

Joseph W. Alba, Editor

MARKETING SCIENCE INSTITUTE

Cambridge, MA 02138 USA

Cover and book design by Laughlin Winkler

Contents

Foreword

The Marketing Science Institute has a long-standing interest in consumer behavior. Customer insights have been consistently identified as a key research priority by our member company trustees. In recent years, there have been profound changes in the marketing landscape. These changes led managers to ask: What are enduring insights about consumer judgments and behavior?

Answering this question posed special challenges. There is a vast amount of research on consumer behavior, spread across diverse academic disciplines, and difficult for a non-expert to access. We consulted with MSI's Advisory Committee, which was formed in 2009 to provide guidance to staff on the best ways to deliver benefits to members. They confirmed our feeling that there was a need for a succinct summary of key insights about consumer behavior—that is, insights based on rigorous and robust research that are useful to managers.

Our proposed structure for the book was based on *Empirical Generalizations about Marketing Impact*, edited by Dominique (Mike) Hanssens. That volume, which MSI published in 2009, has been very well received, and we believed that a book on consumer insights could likewise become an important reference tool for thoughtful marketers. We are grateful to Mike for his work on *Empirical Generalizations*.

We invited Joseph Alba of the University of Florida to take on the role of editor. A highly cited author, Joe has great breadth and depth of knowledge on consumer behavior topics. His expertise includes consumer recall, knowledge, expertise, and learning; price discounts, evaluations, and fairness; and brand salience, extensions, and competition, as well as the effects of contextual cues on consumer judgments. We felt that he would be singularly well suited to the challenge of developing and editing the book.

Each topic in the current volume includes a brief discussion of consumer insight or insights followed by a description of the evidence base, managerial implications, and selected references.

Joe refined the conceptual framework, identified the topics, and provided editorial direction for the book. He selected an impressive group of subject matter experts, who developed the entries in this volume under his supervision. With thanks for his in-sightful work, we are delighted to present the result, *Consumer Insights: Findings from Behavioral Research.*

Ruth Bolton
Marketing Science Institute
Executive Director 2009–11

Introduction

This volume was inspired by its MSI predecessor, *Empirical Generalizations about Marketing Impact,* in which Dominique Hanssens of UCLA catalogued a set of managerially relevant generalizations derived from basic research.

When Ruth Bolton approached me to organize a comparable effort focusing on the contributions made by behavioral scientists, the idea did not immediately resonate. As scientists, our inclination has not been to understand the "main effects" of consumer behavior but rather to paint a complete picture of a phenomenon that includes its numerous and nuanced moderators and higher-order interactions—a laudable objective, but one that may run counter to pragmatic utility.

As I reflected on Ruth's request, however, I became curious. Behavioral research has been engaged in sustained pursuit of many interesting topics. How many of these topics currently lend themselves to a confidently expressed empirical generalization? The scholars I contacted to address the question initially shared my reaction, but in the end they—individually and collectively—produced an answer: this book. I hope that readers will be heartened by the outcome. It should be apparent that many of the topics we explore incrementally contain big-picture implications for practice.

Two points are worth noting with regard to content. First, the topics tend to be less problem-oriented than those included in its predecessor. Behavioral research frequently tries to understand fundamental properties of consumer behavior, the applications of which can span multiple decision contexts and marketing activities. Wherever possible, the chapters have been organized around traditional marketing functions, but in some instances, the implications of a line of research are more diffuse. In these instances, the reader is left to draw connections between a phenomenon and its diverse managerial applications.

Second, to be included in this volume, a topic required a sufficiently large literature on which to base a generalization. Many intriguing topics currently under investigation are not represented but will likely merit a generalization in the future. Contrariwise, there undoubtedly are other topics that should have been included. Omissions were inadvertent but nonetheless my responsibility.

I wish to express my gratitude to Ruth for allowing me the opportunity to participate in this project, to Susan Keane for her generous assistance in its production, and to the authors for their scholarship and goodwill.

Joe Alba

Information Search

1

Effects of Product Knowledge on Information Search

Consumers search for information to improve their decision outcomes, to increase confidence in their decisions, and sometimes just to enjoy the shopping process. In general, the effect of consumer knowledge on the amount of information search is a function of (1) complexity of the purchase, (2) whether that knowledge is objective or self-assessed, and (3) the consumer's level of interest in the product category.

Complexity of the purchase decision

Complex purchase decisions involve many attractive options that differ significantly in their relative benefits. When the purchase decision is relatively complex, the level of consumer product knowledge has two major offsetting effects: facilitating and efficiency effects.

Knowledge *facilitates* information search because knowledgeable consumers can:
- Acquire and understand new information since the terminology is familiar.
- Identify what information is needed since they are aware of potential problems and requirements of various usage situations.

Knowledge leads to higher *efficiency* in searching because knowledgeable consumers can:
- Rely on pre-existing knowledge about potential purchase options rather than having to acquire all new information.
- Screen out unimportant information.
- Recognize alternatives that do not meet the needs of the usage situation, and filter these out early in the decision process.

Because of these offsetting effects, the empirical relationship between knowledge levels and the amount of information search in a particular purchase scenario may be positive, negative, or inverted-U-shaped. In relatively simple purchase situations, efficiency effects are likely to dominate. In contrast, in highly complex environments (e.g., new technology), the facilitating effect may dominate.

Consumer level of interest

Knowledge is intertwined with motivation factors, especially product and purchase involvement. When consumers have an enduring interest in the purchase category (e.g., fashion, travel, or electronics), they are likely to seek product information on an ongoing basis. When a purchase occasion arises, they typically enjoy the opportunity to acquire more information, and their high knowledge levels facilitate their doing so.

Objective versus self-assessed knowledge

Experts tend to overrate their knowledge in complex situations, while novices tend to underrate theirs in straightforward situations. Thus, consumer self-assessments of knowledge may not be a valid measure of actual consumer knowledge levels.

Evidence Base

Compilation of dozens of academic papers using controlled laboratory studies and surveys of self-reported search behavior. Conceptual bases are drawn from theoretical research in psychology and economics.

Managerial Implications

Consumer knowledge is a key segmentation variable for product categories character- ized by many attributes and trade-offs among key benefits. When the product category is complex, consumers lacking in product knowledge may conduct limited informa- tion searches, leading to sub-optimal decision outcomes and subsequent dissatisfaction with the purchase. Managers should research the obstacles faced by low-knowledge consumers and find creative ways to overcome them (e.g., color-coding systems for usage situations, salesperson training for appropriate vocabulary, etc.). Consumers who are highly knowledgeable may choose to rely on information they already pos- sess rather than searching extensively. Marketers should seek to make highly knowl- edgeable consumers aware of new information and options.

Contributor

Merrie Brucks, University of Arizona

References

Beatty, Sharon E., and Scott Smith (1987), "External Search Effort: An Investigation Across Several Product Categories." *Journal of Consumer Research* 14 (June), 83–95.

Bloch, Peter H., Daniel L. Sherrell, and Nancy M. Ridgway (1986), "Consumer Search: An Extended Framework." *Journal of Consumer Research* 13 (June), 119–26.

Brucks, Merrie (1985), "The Effects of Product Class Knowledge on Information Search Behavior." *Journal of Consumer Research* 12 (June), 1–16.

2

In-store Decision Making and Unplanned Purchases

Insights

Research spanning 30 years indicates that the ratio of unplanned to planned purchases has remained approximately 2:1. Paradoxically, shoppers are able to predict their overall trip spend relatively accurately, despite the fact that over half of their purchase decisions are made in-store. This accuracy is due to shoppers' use of a mental budget allocated for in-store decisions ("in-store slack").

Consumers' use of in-store slack and promotional savings encountered during the trip interact in the following ways:

- *Before* slack is depleted (that is, before consumers have spent the portion of their mental budget allocated for in-store decisions), promotional savings on planned items increase planned item spending. High-income shoppers draw from their in-store slack to stockpile promoted planned items, while lower-income shoppers draw from their slack to switch to higher-tier brands of planned items. Before slack is depleted, promotional savings on unplanned items do not increase unplanned item spending.
- *After* slack is depleted, promotional savings on *both planned and unplanned* items increase unplanned item spending. This is because shoppers use the savings on planned items to make unplanned purchases. After slack is depleted, promotional savings on planned items do not increase spending on planned items.

Four types of factors are associated with unplanned spending:

- Category: Unplanned purchasing is greater for categories that are more hedonic, less frequently purchased, and on display.
- Shopper demographics: Women, larger households, and higher-income households make more unplanned purchases on a given shopping trip.
- Shopper behaviors and trip factors: Paying by credit card, shopping more aisles, not using a list, spending more time in-store, and shopping less frequently are associated with more unplanned purchases on a given shopping trip.
- Shopper psychological states/factors: Greater store familiarity, more abstract shopping goals, and greater impulsiveness/compulsiveness are associated with more unplanned purchases on a given shopping trip.

Evidence Base

Compilation across six academic studies, all conducted in the field.

Managerial Implications

Managers can spur unplanned purchases in the following ways:

- Encouraging consumers to shop more aisles and be exposed to more product categories and in-store displays.
- Arranging aisles based on consumers' prior knowledge or expectations of product location.
- Displaying frequently purchased or "destination" categories next to less frequently purchased products. This is particularly useful when categories with longer interpurchase cycles are usage complements to products with shorter interpurchase cycles (e.g., canned tuna and mayonnaise).
- Making the shopping experience as pleasant as possible to increase time spent in the store.
- Persuading shoppers to evoke abstract goals (e.g., Wal-Mart's "Save Money. Live Better" slogan).
- Placing stockpiling-inducing promotions (e.g., buy-one-get-one-free promotions) earlier in the typical store traffic pattern. These promotions should be focused on items that tend to be planned, such as yogurt or bottled water.
- Offering promotions on planned items later in the store pattern. Displays of products that tend to be unplanned should be placed near promotions of these planned items.
- Using frequent-shopper program data to identify categories/brands with a higher penetration of higher-income households and adding a secondary location later in the typical trip path.

Contributor
J. Jeffrey Inman, University of Pittsburgh

References

Bell, David R., Daniel Corsten, and George Knox (2011), "From Point of Purchase to Path to Purchase: How Preshopping Factors Drive Unplanned Buying." *Journal of Marketing* 75 (January), 31–45.

Inman, J. Jeffrey, Russell S. Winer, and Rosellina Ferraro (2009), "In-Store Decision Making: The Role of Category-Level and Shopping Trip-Level Factors." *Journal of Marketing* 73 (September), 19–29.

Kollat, David T., and Ronald P. Willett (1967), "Customer Impulse Purchasing Behavior." *Journal of Marketing Research* 4 (February), 21–31.

Stilley, Karen M., J. Jeffrey Inman, and Kirk L. Wakefield (2010), "Spending on the Fly: Mental Budgets, Promotions, and Spending Behavior." *Journal of Marketing* 74 (May), 34–47.

3

Perceptions of Product Assortment

Insights

Offering a greater number of products increases consumers' assortment perceptions. However, perceptions of product assortment are not simply a one-to-one function of the number of product options offered in a category. Holding the number of products constant, consumer assortment perceptions can also be increased by:

- Offering more preferred products.
- Offering more unique attributes and alternatives.
- Offering more variability on important attributes.
- Increasing the size of the product display.
- Organizing the product display to match consumer mental categories and shopping goals.

Higher perceived assortment has been shown to lead to greater amounts consumed. However, larger assortments can be a double-edged sword when consumers must choose a single product. Consumer choice from a product assortment is a two-stage hierarchical process, with large product assortments initially attracting consumers to a retailer but subsequently hindering consumers' selection of a final product.

Consumers find large assortments attractive for their process-related benefits of stimulation, choice freedom, and informative value, as well as for their choice-related benefits of higher ideal product availability, ability to satisfy multiple needs in a single location, potential for variety seeking, and flexibility for uncertain future preferences. Yet, consumers with less-developed product preferences are more likely to be overwhelmed by large product assortments and suffer negative consequences, such as lower choice accuracy, lower satisfaction, higher regret, and higher deferral of choice.

Evidence Base

Compilation of 50 academic papers, reporting over 100 empirical studies. Evidence base is mostly laboratory based, although it includes several field studies.

Managerial Implications

Smaller product sets may be perceived as offering greater assortment than larger product sets if the smaller set includes more preferred products, more unique products, greater variability on important attributes, and greater shelf display space.

Generally, shelf organization leads to higher assortment perceptions, as it facilitates consumers processing all the product options. However, when the number of products is small, organization facilitates recognition that the offering is limited and, consequently, a disorganized organization may lead to higher perceptions of assortment. Further, shelf organization has been shown to interact with consumer knowledge and shopping goals. Consumers who are familiar with a product category perceive higher assortment when the shelf organization matches their internal category representations (e.g., organized by brand for brand-oriented consumers rather than by product type). For consumers who have low familiarity with the category, assortment perceptions are higher when the organization matches their situation shopping goals (e.g., used cars organized by miles per gallon for consumers looking to reduce fuel expenses).

Consumers with well-developed (versus less-developed) preferences are most likely to enjoy the benefits of a large assortment without negative decision-making consequences. To assist consumers with less-developed preferences, managers can offer decision aids where consumers assess their attribute preferences and formulate trade-offs on the relative importance of these attributes prior to choosing from an assortment.

Individual differences also affect consumer decision making from product assortments. Consumers who exhibit a "maximizer" tendency, with the goal of choosing the absolute best product, encounter greater choice difficulty and higher regret with choosing from a large assortment than "satisficing" consumers who have the goal of simply choosing an acceptable product.

Contributor
Susan M. Broniarczyk, University of Texas at Austin

References

Broniarczyk, Susan M. (2008), "Product Assortment." In *Handbook of Consumer Psychology*, eds. Curtis P. Haugtvedt, Paul M. Herr, and Frank R. Kardes, 755–79. New York, N.Y.: Lawrence Erlbaum Associates.

Chernev, Alexander (2003), "Product Assortment and Individual Decision Processes." *Journal of Personality and Social Psychology* 85 (July), 151–62.

Iyengar, Sheena, and Mark Lepper (2000), "When Choice Is Demotivating: Can One Desire Too Much of a Good Thing?" *Journal of Personality and Social Psychology* 79 (December), 995–1006.

4

Variety-seeking Behavior

Variety-seeking behavior has been defined as the vacillation of choice among an acceptable set of alternatives over time. It can occur as a result of external motivation; for example, social influences, varying situations or contexts, or differing goals can increase or decrease variety-seeking behavior.

Variety-seeking behavior can also occur because of the intrinsic desire for change due to the need for increased stimulation, or to overcome boredom or satiation. That is, consumers may choose to switch among alternatives, rather than repeat consumption of favored items, because of the pleasure they derive from the change itself. Consumers switch among these familiar alternatives, not because their preferences change, but just because they want something different.

Variety-seeking behavior may also occur as a hedge against future uncertainty. Finally, people may choose variety because of a belief that variety seeking will help them resolve a choice that is otherwise difficult. Thus, consumers may choose variety as a mechanism to avoid having to make difficult trade-offs.

Some key findings are:
- Consumers expect others to evaluate their decision more favorably if they choose variety in cultures where self-expression and uniqueness are valued (e.g., in the U.S.). This is less true in collectivist cultures.
- Moderate or mild positive affect increases variety seeking when circumstances do not make unpleasant or negative features of the items in the choice task salient. However, extreme positive moods can decrease variety seeking.
- Hunger and visual food cues enhance variety seeking in food categories.
- Consumers will sometimes balance their need for variety by choosing more variety in one category and less variety in another. Further, spatially confined consumers may react against an incursion on their personal space by choosing more variety.
- Consumers sometimes choose "too much variety"; in other words, they choose a set of choices in which they include items that they like less than other items they could

have chosen. For example, an arbitrary dimension such as the way the choice set is framed or partitioned can affect the final choice of items. Consumers are more likely to choose a more varied sequence of items when considering the items as a portfolio of choices than when considering each of the offerings in isolation.

- Consumers choose more variety when they choose several items at one time or on one shopping trip for future consumption than if they make separate choices immediately preceding consumption.
- If consumers will be evaluating their choices retrospectively, they will favor sequences that include more variety. For example, if people are trying to shape their memory of a vacation, they will include more varied activities, even if these activities include those that are less desirable while being consumed in real time.
- There are individual differences in how much people value variety. People who are high self-monitors or have high optimal stimulation levels prefer more variety.
- There are also product class differences. Consumers are more likely to switch between sensory attributes (e.g., flavor) than non-sensory attributes (e.g., brand). The incidence of variety seeking is greater in product categories where packaging is similar among competitors, as compared to categories where the packaging is less uniform across brands.

Evidence Base

A compilation of over 50 academic papers, including 6 review papers, reporting over 100 empirical studies. The evidence base is panel data studies and laboratory-based experiments with both real and hypothetical outcomes and varies by insight (ranging from 2 to 25+ studies).

Managerial Implications

- Increasing consumers' needs for variety increases the market share of the least-preferred brand and decreases the market share of the most-preferred one.
- When variety seeking is encouraged, positioning a brand to seem more similar to others is likely to lead to a loss in market share.
- The more frequently and intensely a consumer uses a product, the more quickly he or she will feel satiated. In such categories, such as soft drinks or shampoos, promoting a brand as a "change of pace" can be successful.
- To increase the desire for stimulation, managers should increase the positive feelings a consumer experiences in the purchase environment and decrease general uncertainty in the purchasing decision.
- To maintain brand loyalty in environments where variety-seeking behavior is observed, managers can provide different flavors or sub-brands to satisfy the need for change while maintaining the loyalty to a brand.

Contributor

Barbara E. Kahn, University of Pennsylvania

References

Kahn, Barbara E. (1995), "Consumer Variety-Seeking among Goods and Services." *Journal of Retailing and Consumer Services* 2 (July), 139–48.

Kahn, Barbara E. (1998), "Variety: From the Consumer Perspective." In *Research Advances in Variety Management*, eds. Christopher S. Tang and Tech H. Ho, 19–37. Boston, Mass.: Kluwer.

Kahn, Barbara E. (1998), "Dynamic Relationships with Customers: High-Variety Strategies." *Journal of the Academy of Marketing Science* 26 (Winter), 45–53.

Kahn, Barbara E., and Rebecca Ratner (2005), "Variety for the Sake of Variety? Diversification Motives in Consumer Choice." In *Inside Consumption: Frontiers of Research on Consumer Motives, Goals, and Desires*, eds. S. Ratneshwar and David Glen Mick, 102–21. London, U.K.: Routledge.

5

Consumer Search on the Internet

It was widely believed that the Internet would produce greater consumer search and increased market efficiency, in some cases eroding profit and causing cutthroat price competition. This has not happened widely, for a number of reasons:

- Using an e-tailer builds familiarity with the interface, and this produces switching costs. Consumers, once they become familiar with a site, are less likely to switch to another provider.
- Choice architecture refers to the myriad of design decisions—including order, number, and display of options and attributes—that can influence search and therefore choice. For example, sorting by price increases price sensitivity, while sorting by quality lessens price sensitivity and increases sensitivity to quality. These effects can persist outside the store because of loyalty to the originally chosen brand. In another example, having a preselected option will lead shoppers to concentrate on that option and search other options less, and the use of no-action default options results in more choice of the default option.
- Firm reputation limits search. Unknown entrants are seen as riskier and less likely to be visited.
- Consumers do not seem to be making rational trade-offs between search time and cost savings.
- Consumer decision making is different for search and experience goods. While information is more important for search goods, user reviews are more important for experience goods.

Evidence Base

Over 20 studies published in the last 10 years. Some are laboratory based, but many are based on field experiments conducted on firm websites or analysis of existing clickstream data provided by firms. Analytic models also provide insights.

Managerial Implications

- Firms can make their digital offerings more attractive by both active and passive learning about the consumer: Active learning means learning tastes by asking the consumer questions so that the right product can be recommended. Passive learning means watching the consumer shop and modifying the interface so that it fits the consumer better.
- Managers should realize that websites are an opportunity to build customer loyalty. Ease of use can be more important in retaining customers.
- Managers can use choice architecture to change what is searched and sold on electronic storefronts. For example, they may use defaults that will be consistent with consumers' preferences.
- Backgrounds, alternative and attribute sorting, and the way attributes are presented can change search behavior and choice and deserve consideration and, when possible, testing.

Contributor
Eric J. Johnson, Columbia University

References

Johnson, Eric J., Steven Bellman, Gerald L. Lohse, and Naomi Mandel (2005), "Designing Marketplaces of the Artificial: Four Approaches to Understanding Consumer Behavior in Electronic Environments." *Journal of Interactive Marketing* 20 (1), 21–33.

Johnson, Eric, Susanne Shu, Benedict Dellaert, Craig Fox, Daniel G. Goldstein, Gerald Haubl, Richard Larrick, John Payne, David Schkade, Brian Wansink, and Elke Weber (in press), "Beyond Nudges: Tools of a Choice Architecture." *Marketing Letters.*

Lal, Rajiv, and Miklos Sarvary (1999), "When and How Is the Internet Likely to Decrease Price Competition." *Marketing Science* 18 (4), 485–503.

6

Buyers' Post-purchase Information Biases

One of the oldest and most robust findings in consumer behavior is the biased use of information *after a product decision* in order to bolster the buyer's choice. Consumers bias post-choice information so that they can defend the wisdom of their product decision. It helps them feel more confident that they chose the right product and leads to fewer second thoughts. Maybe just as important, these biases impose no cost on choice accuracy because the product decision has already been made.

This bias shows up in two forms, one with a long history, the other newly demonstrated. The more familiar is "selective exposure to information," in which buyers select additional information that confirms their choice and reject information that might disconfirm it. As long ago as 1957, Ehrlich et al. found that new car buyers tended to read more advertisements for the car they had just purchased than for the cars they had considered but decided not to buy.

The second form of the decision-bolstering bias is distorting the evaluation of whatever information is acquired. This distortion makes the information seem more supportive of the chosen product than it otherwise would, whether that information was deliberately sought or just encountered.

Evidence Base

Meta-analysis of 91 selective exposure studies published over more than 50 years, and 3 recent laboratory-based studies.

Managerial Implications

Yogi Berra famously said, "It ain't over till it's over." These research results suggest, "And it ain't over even then." What makes buyers' post-purchase bias valuable for marketers is both that it supports the purchase (always a good thing) and that it is *self-generated*. Because buyers select the information that they themselves want and then interpret that information as they personally see it, they "own" their product-supporting conclusions. They believe these positive evaluations of their purchased products much more than if they had only read or heard the same information.

This leads to the following implications:
- Managers should find ways to follow through after a recent purchase, whether the buyer is a loyal customer or not. When managers provide opportunities for recent purchasers to obtain additional information, buyers are likely to talk themselves into a stronger brand preference.
- Managers should follow through as soon as possible after the purchase while the commitment to the product remains strong. The stronger is this commitment, the stronger is the bias to support the purchased product.
- Once buyers have made the product decision, it's over—but then it's not. Some purchases can be returned, some need follow-through on product assembly or usage, and some may never be repurchased when they could be. Every case is an opportunity for the marketer to strengthen the product preference. And buyers' natural post-choice biases will help do that.
- Buyers talk to other buyers. Managers should give them more opportunities to follow up their purchase and, thereby, more to talk about. Then, in conversations with their friends, the post-choice bias will naturally prompt positive statements about the purchased product that are genuinely believed and, therefore, genuinely believable.

Contributor
J. Edward Russo, Cornell University

References
Ehrlich, Danuta, Isaiah Guttman, Peter Schonbach, and Judson Mills (1957), "Postdecision Exposure to Relevant Information." *Journal of Abnormal and Social Psychology* 54 (1), 98–102.

Hart, William, Dolores Albarracin, Alice Eagly, Inge Brechan, Matthew J. Lindberg, and Lisa Merrill (2009), "Feeling Validated Versus Being Correct: A Meta-analysis of Selective Exposure to Information." *Psychological Bulletin* 135 (4), 555–88.

Russo, J. Edward, Neda Kerimi, and Anne-Sophie Chaxel (2011), "Preference-driven Biases in Consumers' Search and Evaluation of Product Information." Ithaca, N.Y.: Cornell University, Working paper.

Pricing

7

Perceptions of Price Deals

Insights

Managers offer price deals all the time. The consumer's perception of price savings from a deal is affected by how the deal is presented as well as the actual discount offered. Many research studies focus on "price framing," that is, how the offer is communicated to the consumer (e.g., Is the offered price given along with a reference price? Is a price deal communicated in dollar or percent terms?). Other studies focus on "situational effects" (e.g., Is the deal within a discount store or a specialty store? Is it for a national brand or a private brand?). Together, these studies offer the following insights.

Price framing
- Both the dollar and the percent amount of the deal positively influence perception of deal savings.
- Tensile claims such as "savings of up to x%" are perceived to offer significantly lower savings than deals framed in terms of non-tensile (objective) claims (savings of x%).
- The presence of a regular price as an external reference price increases perceived deal savings. However, when the deal percentage or amount is extremely large, consumers may deflate the external reference price when they observe a sale.
- "Implausibility" of a deal makes it less attractive. However, a large deal amount more than compensates for its lower plausibility, so that deals of large magnitudes are evaluated more favorably than deals of smaller magnitudes.
- Within-store price frames (e.g., current price is x, our regular price is y) are more effective when the consumer is shopping, but between-store price frames (e.g., our price is x, competing store's price is y) are more effective when communicating with consumers at home.
- Presenting manufacturer-suggested price is more credible for national brands than for other brands.
- Consumers value savings on bundles less as the bundle size increases, that is, small bundles with high-percentage discounts are most impactful for consumers. This could be because consumers average the savings by the number of items.

Situational effects

- Deals on national brands are evaluated more favorably than deals on private brands and generics.
- Consumers value deals less in stores that have higher deal frequency (discount stores) compared to stores perceived to have lower deal frequency (e.g., specialty stores).
- Deals are more effective if they are less consistent (less predictable) and more distinctive.
- Including free gifts in general lowers the perceived value of the deal.

Evidence Base

Meta-analysis of 345 observations from 30 studies across 20 articles published in marketing. These studies used laboratory experiments where deal evaluation was actually measured as opposed to inferred.

Managerial Implications

- What works for your competitors may or may not work for you. For instance, listing the manufacturer-suggested price in a point-of-purchase promotion sign may work for a national brand, but not for a local brand.
- While both deal percent and deal amount positively influence perceived deal savings, deal percent has more impact—with fixed budgets, choose to give deals where the % deal is bigger.
- Managers should announce the regular price for high-value deals, but not for low-value deals.
- Managers should use between-store reference price frames (e.g., current price is x, our regular price is y) for print and TV ads that consumers will view outside the store, but within-store frames (e.g., our price is x, competing store's price is y) at the point-of-purchase.
- Managers should not worry too much that implausible-sounding deals will backfire. Consumers will discount such deals, but they will still have a positive impact on sales.

Contributor
Aradhna Krishna, University of Michigan

Reference
Krishna, Aradhna, Richard Briesch, Donald Lehmann, and Hong Yuan (2002), "A Meta-Analysis of the Impact of Price Presentation on Perceived Savings." *Journal of Retailing* 78 (2), 101–18.

8

Biases in Processing Price Information

Consumers do not always perfectly process price information and are sometimes prone to biases. These biases in turn can affect how consumers react to prices and their subsequent demand for products. Some of these biases are:

Anchoring biases

Consumers anchor on the left-most digits of prices, which can lead them to underestimate the magnitude of 9-ending prices (i.e., $7.99 may seem much cheaper than $8.00).

When a price is divided into multiple mandatory parts (e.g., base price plus shipping and handling), consumers often anchor on the base price, do not fully account for surcharges, and therefore underestimate total purchase costs.

Price association biases

Consumers associate 9-ending prices (e.g., $7.99) with being on sale or being a good deal and associate round prices with higher quality ($8.00).

Consumers are influenced by incidental product prices (e.g., prices for products adjacent to the ones they are considering buying), even when those products are neither being considered nor a relevant basis for comparison.

Consumers judge the price level of a store based on how many of its products have low prices and how low the prices are, but they often place more weight on frequency than on depth. Thus, consumers perceive a store to be cheaper when it has many moderately low-priced products compared to when it has a few extremely low-priced ones.

Price magnitude biases

Consumers misattribute the magnitude of a price difference to the ease or difficulty of computing the difference between two prices. That is, they tend to think that easy-to-calculate differences (e.g., $5.00–$4.00) are larger in magnitude than more difficult-to-calculate differences ($4.97–$3.96), holding the actual magnitude of the difference constant.

Similarly, consumers' judgments about the magnitude of a price are influenced by the precision or roundedness of prices. That is, they tend to perceive precise prices ($395,425) to be lower in magnitude than round prices (e.g., $395,000) of similar actual magnitude.

Consumers' judgments about the magnitude of a price are influenced by the physical size of the price representation. Consumers therefore perceive a price to be lower when the price is represented in smaller rather than in larger font.

Evidence Base

Compilation of over 20 academic papers, reporting over 60 empirical studies, primarily laboratory experiments conducted with student samples.

Managerial Implications

- Managers should understand that consumers do not always accurately process price information.
- Managers should use their knowledge of consumer biases to construct prices that meet their goals. They should understand pricing decisions go beyond price magnitude, for example, that pricing digits, precision, and display fonts can also affect consumers' price perceptions.
- Managers should understand that consumers' perception of the price of a particular target product may be biased by incidental prices and by overall store pricing.

Contributor
Vicki G. Morwitz, New York University

References

Monroe, Kent B. (2003), *Pricing: Making Profitable Decisions*. New York, N.Y.: McGraw-Hill/Irwin.

Raghubir, Priya (2006), "An Information Processing Review of the Subjective Value of Money and Prices." *Journal of Business Research* 59 (October), 1053–62.

Thomas, Manoj, and Vicki G. Morwitz (2009), "Heuristics in Numerical Cognition: Implications for Pricing." In *Handbook of Research in Pricing*, ed. Vithala Rao, 132–49. Cheltenham, U.K.: Edward Elgar Publishing.

Winer, Russell S. (1988), "Behavioral Perspectives on Pricing: Buyers' Subjective Perceptions of Price Revisited." In *Issues in Pricing: Theory and Research*, ed. Timothy Devinney. Lexington, Mass.: Lexington Books.

9

Effects of the Internet on Consumer Price Sensitivity

Insights

The Internet can change consumer price sensitivity by making it easier to search for a particular SKU, for price, and for preference-relevant features. Despite many forecasts in the 1990s, adoption of online shopping has not led to increased price sensitivity and price competition, except for homogenous goods where competing sellers are offering exactly the same items. For differentiated goods, lowered search costs affect consumers by changing the weight of price and quality information about considered brands or by changing consumers' consideration sets.

Price sensitivity and lower search cost for information about considered brands

Unsurprisingly, lower search costs for price information online increase price sensitivity. Less appreciated is that lower search costs for quality online make consumers see bigger differences in utility, decreasing price sensitivity.

Easier comparison across stores increases price sensitivity for identical items sold at multiple stores. But when goods differ on dimensions in addition to price, easy comparison does not lead to heightened price sensitivity, because trade-offs are complex. Branding, differentiation, and consumer loyalty continue to play a key role in online shopping. If consumers see large differences among retailers, they engage in little search.

Price sensitivity and consideration set size and composition

Lower search costs for locating alternatives should increase average consideration set size, and larger consideration sets increase price sensitivity. However, this effect has proved much weaker than expected because people search only a little more online than offline.

The more important effect on consideration sets comes from screening via "recommendation agents." If screened options list the best-fitting ones at the top of a list, alternatives in the consumer's consideration set will be more similar in overall utility than if consumers search without effective screening. Thus, consumers find better-fitting options without paying more, or opt to pay more for much more consumption utility. Sellers do not necessarily have an incentive to provide screening; they do so only if they make more money by doing so than by withholding this information.

Effects on markets

By matching buyers with unusual tastes with sellers of products matching those tastes, the Internet can create new markets. It can also increase competition between buyers when consumers buy via auctions rather than traditional retail formats. For example, buyers can access information about a product ahead of the auction event. They can also select the most relevant auctions to attend, thereby increasing competition among buyers, and leading to fewer rejected bids. Sellers have increased expected revenues from buyers due to this efficiency.

Evidence Base

Compilation of over 50 academic papers, including laboratory and field experiments, econometric analyses, and analytical models.

Managerial Implications

- Because easy comparison can heighten price sensitivity for identical products, retailers' incentives to carry different SKUs than their competitors are greater on the Internet than in an older, bricks-and-mortar world. For example, retailers have increased incentives to replace national brands with private labels.
- Manufacturers can counteract the lost market share to private labels by creating retailer-specific "branded variants" that have slight differences from other models of the same product available in the marketplace.
- Branding and loyalty are just as important to reducing price sensitivity in Internet retailing as in a bricks-and-mortar world. For online retailers, technological elements of the site can lead to loyalty; such elements might include ease of learning the interface or superior ability to screen products to find those that best fit a consumer's preferences.

Contributors

John G. Lynch, Jr., University of Colorado at Boulder, and Florian Zettelmeyer, Northwestern University

References

Alba, Joseph, John Lynch, Barton Weitz, Chris Janiszewski, Richard Lutz, Alan Sawyer, and Stacy Wood (1997), "Interactive Home Shopping: Consumer, Retailer, and Manufacturer Incentives to Participate in Electronic Marketplaces." *Journal of Marketing* 61 (July), 38–53.

Diehl, Kristin, Laura J. Kornish, and John G. Lynch, Jr. (2003), "Smart Agents: When Lower Search Costs for Quality Information Increase Price Sensitivity." *Journal of Consumer Research* 30 (June), 56–71.

Lynch, John G., Jr., and Dan Ariely (2000), "Wine Online: Search Costs and Competition on Price, Quality, and Distribution." *Marketing Science* 19 (1), 83–103.

Zettelmeyer, Florian, Fiona Scott Morton, and Jorge Silva-Risso (2006), "How the Internet Lowers Prices: Evidence from Matched Survey and Auto Transaction Data." *Journal of Marketing Research* 43 (2), 168–81.

10

Effects of Transaction Structure on Price Perceptions and Consumption

Insights

Consumers paying for a product or service set up a mental account in which the negative value of the price paid, the so-called "pain of payment," is associated (coupled) with the positive value of the opportunity to consume the product or service. Consumption is driven by the need to offset the pain of payment with the benefit from consuming. However, the manner in which a transaction is structured can loosen the coupling between price and consumption and can affect consumption patterns. Coupling is weakened in two ways: transaction decoupling and payment depreciation.

Transaction decoupling

The format of a transaction can make it difficult to associate a dollar value with each unit of consumption. Examples include bundled products and services, payment by credit cards, or purchases of multiple units (e.g., a volume pack or a season ticket for sporting events). When the association between a unit of consumption and its price is decoupled, the unit of consumption is undervalued and the pain of payment is lowered. In the extreme, the unit of consumption is perceived as a free good. For tangible products, this results in greater consumption and for services, a greater likelihood of foregoing a paid-for opportunity.

Payment depreciation

After prepayment for goods or services, consumers gradually adapt to the pain of payment. In their mental account, the negative value of the payment declines with time, and hence a smaller positive value is required to offset the pain of payment. For tangible products, this results in greater consumption and for services, a greater likelihood of foregoing a paid-for opportunity. Examples of payment depreciation include subscription services with one annual payment, theater tickets with advance purchases, and stockpiled non-perishable food items purchased in advance. In the context of health clubs, results show that attendance declines the further away in time one goes from payment.

Evidence Base

Compilation of 15 academic papers, reporting over 50 empirical studies. This evidence base includes a mix of laboratory studies, analysis of archived data, field experiments, and survey data.

Managerial Implications

There are many situations in which marketers need to manage consumption. A marketer of packaged goods might want to accelerate product consumption, the manager of a health club might want to ensure that patrons are using the facilities at the end of the year to increase their likelihood of renewing, and a provider of healthcare insurance might want to encourage an annual medical checkup.

In the first case, a marketer might employ transaction decoupling or payment depreciation strategies to encourage consumption. Since these strategies will result in lower consumption of services, in the latter cases, a marketer might make the pain of payment more, rather than less, salient. The pain of payment can be highlighted by specifying a dollar value of each benefit in a bundle, using payment mechanisms like cash or check rather than credit or debit cards, and making the payment salient close in time to the service opportunity.

Contributor
Dilip Soman, University of Toronto

References

Gourville, John, and Dilip Soman (2002), "Pricing and the Psychology of Consumption." *Harvard Business Review* (September), 90–6.

Soman, Dilip, and John Gourville (2001), "Transaction Decoupling: How Price Bundling Affects the Decision to Consume." *Journal of Marketing Research* 38 (February), 30–44.

Thaler, Richard H. (1999), "Mental Accounting Matters." *Journal of Behavioral Decision Making* 12 (September), 183–206.

11

Perceptions of Price Fairness

Insights

Perceived fairness of vendors' prices will influence consumers' attitudes and purchase intentions. Consumers judge fairness by comparing the sticker price to salient reference points that include the previously encountered price for the product, competitors' prices, estimated cost of product production, and prices paid by other consumers. These reference points can generate ill will for several reasons:

- First, consumers underestimate the effects of inflation, which can lead to "sticker shock." Price increases that reflect changes in supply and demand are deemed exploitive, and consumers may attribute seller price differences primarily to profit-seeking rather than differential costs.
- Consumers tend to underestimate vendors' costs, in part because the multitude of costs incurred by vendors—particularly overhead costs—are opaque to consumers. Even when informed of costs, consumers view some costs (e.g., promotional costs) less favorably than others (e.g., variable material costs).
- Consumers anchor fair prices for goods on material costs (i.e., cost of goods sold). However, sellers of a pure service may be viewed as having negligible costs, which drives the estimated "fair" price downward.
- Controlling for the magnitude of total profit, different profit models elicit different perceptions of fairness. (For example, margin strategies are perceived as less fair than volume strategies.) Price differences across vendors are deemed fairest if they can be attributed to differences in product quality. Paying a different price (whether higher or lower) than another customer is seen as unfair. Consequently, perceived fairness acts as a constraint on dynamic pricing.

Evidence Base

Compilation of 21 academic papers, reporting over 60 empirical studies. Evidence base is mostly laboratory based and varies by insight (ranging from 2 to 25+ studies).

Managerial Implications

- Managers should actively manage price expectations by establishing credible reference points and encouraging favorable comparisons.
- Managers should differentiate to reduce comparability when comparisons are unfavorable.
- Managers should actively manage perceptions of costs by focusing attention on all costs of production, especially material costs and non-volitional costs.
- Managers should emphasize quality (and underlying differences in costs of production) to overcome unfavorable price comparisons and enhance perceptions of price fairness.

Contributors

Lisa E. Bolton, Pennsylvania State University, and Joseph W. Alba, University of Florida

References

Bolton, Lisa E., Luk Warlop, and Joseph W. Alba (2003), "Consumer Perceptions of Price (Un)Fairness." *Journal of Consumer Research* 29 (March), 474–91.

Kahneman, Daniel, Jack L. Knetsch, and Richard H. Thaler (1986), "Fairness as a Constraint on Profit Seeking: Entitlements in the Market." *American Economic Review* 76 (September), 728–41.

Xia, Lan, Kent B. Monroe, and Jennifer L. Cox (2004), "The Price Is Unfair! A Conceptual Framework of Price Fairness Perceptions." *Journal of Marketing* 68 (October), 1–15.

Advertising

12

Consumer Attention to Advertising

Insights

Attention is the crucial condition for advertising to be effective. It is the focusing of processing capacity on an object (what) in space (where) and time (when). Attention has two main functions: selection and coordination. Attention selection is the first stage in advertising processing. Attention selects certain ads from among the competition of other ads and the environment, and selects specific objects or locations within the ads at the expense of others. Attention engagement coordinates consumers' information processing and choice behaviors. That is, with attention, consumers learn faster and more efficiently from advertising and make better choices.

There are several robust findings about attention to advertising:

1   Attention to ads is short. Consumers spend much less time on advertising than marketing practitioners and academics commonly believe. Attention to print ads in magazines and feature ads in newspapers is on average 1–2 seconds. This is much less than the 20 or more seconds that are regularly used in marketing research to test ads.

2   Attention can be readily measured with eye-tracking. Visual attention can be easily measured with infrared eye-tracking methodology. This methodology is widely available at relatively low costs and enables precise recordings of visual attention to advertising for large samples of ads and people. In contrast, verbal reports and memory of attention to advertising are unreliable and invalid measures, due to the speed of the attentional processes and the difficulty of cognitively penetrating them.

3   Attention to advertising is under managerial control. Gaze duration on a print ad as a whole increases by 0.8% for every 1% increase in its size (for feature ads, this size elasticity is 0.2%). Attention to the pictorial and brand increase only 0.3% for a 1% increase in their surface sizes. Attention to the text in advertisements, on the other hand, is strongly dependent on the amount of text: a 1% increase in surface size of the text leads to a 0.9% increase in gaze. (This is counter to advertising practice that maximizes the size of pictorials at the expense of the text.)

The visual clutter in advertisements, objectively assessed by the file size of the compressed ad image of a standard resolution (jpeg), reduces attention to the brand and the ad as a whole: a 1% increase in file size reduces attention to the brand by 0.5%.

Attention to retail display ads can be optimized such that all (national brand and private label) feature ads contained in them gain attention. In these optimal configurations, pictorials and text should be smaller, but price and promotion elements should be 60% (respectively 10% larger than current practice).

4 Improvements in attention improve ad effectiveness. Small differences in attention to the brand significantly improve brand memory (a 5% increase in memory for a single eye-fixation on the brand in case of magazine ads). Attention to the ad as a whole can improve sales: adjusted for their size, a 1% increase in attention leads to a 0.3% increase in sales in the case of feature ads.

Evidence Base

Multiple articles reporting research across thousands of magazine ads and hundreds of retail feature ads, collected from multiple samples of regular consumers. Attention is measured with eye-tracking methodology.

Managerial Implications

- Ads should be pretested under everyday short-exposure durations, rather than under artificially long-exposure durations, as is common in ad practice: ads that perform well under high levels of attention may do worse under low levels.
- Because of their wide availability, cost effectiveness, and desirable measurement properties, ad pretesting should include eye-tracking measures of attention.
- To improve attention to ads, less space should be devoted to pictorials and more space to the brand and text in print advertisements.
- To increase attention to the brands in ads, the visual clutter in ads should be reduced; clutter can be simply assessed as the file size of the jpeg ad image.
- Feature display ads of retailers should be optimized as a whole, such that they attract maximum attention to all of the ads for the featured products: this involves reducing the size of pictorials and text, and increasing the size of brand, price, and promotion elements.
- Retailers and brand managers can increase sales of their products without additional advertising costs by increasing consumers' attention to their feature ads.

Contributors
Rik Pieters, Tilburg University, and Michel Wedel, University of Maryland

References

Pieters, Rik, Michel Wedel, and Rajeev Batra (2010), "The Stopping Power of Advertising: Measures and Effects of Visual Complexity." *Journal of Marketing* 74 (5), 48–60.

Pieters, Rik, Michel Wedel, and Jie Zhang (2007), "Optimal Feature Advertising Under Competitive Clutter." *Management Science* 51 (11), 1815–28.

Wedel, Michel, and Rik Pieters (2000), "Eye Fixations on Advertisements and Memory for Brands: A Model and Findings." *Marketing Science* 19 (4), 297–312.

Zhang, Jie, Michel Wedel, and Rik Pieters (2009), "Sales Effects of Attention to Feature Advertisements: A Bayesian Mediation Analysis." *Journal of Marketing Research* 46 (October), 669–81.

13

Effects of Ad Likability

Insights

Ad likability, that is, consumer attitudes toward and feelings generated by an advertisement, "rub off" on the brand being promoted, especially under low-involvement processing conditions. Ad attitude (typically measured using Semantic Differential scales) had median corrected r's of 0.68 and 0.36 with brand attitude and purchase intention, respectively.[1] Under higher involvement conditions, ad attitude has a dual effect; structural equation analysis has demonstrated that in addition to the direct relationship between ad attitude and brand attitude, ad attitude is positively related to brand perceptions that in turn predict brand attitude, an indirect effect of ad attitude.

Ad-generated feelings were also correlated with brand attitudes and purchase intentions. That is, negative ad-generated feelings had mean corrected r's of -0.39, and -0.20 with brand attitude and purchase intention, respectively, while positive feelings showed mean corrected r's (in the same order) of 0.37 and 0.28. Finally, standard copy-test measures of ad likability were strongly predictive of ad campaign sales performance.

Evidence Base

Meta-analysis of 47 separate samples included in 43 academic articles; meta-analysis of 55 studies reported in 46 academic articles; large-scale industry research program.

Managerial Implications

Brand managers and their promotional partners (e.g., ad agencies) should generally aim to construct advertisements that not only communicate relevant brand information but do so in engaging fashion. The positive affect generated by an advertisement influences brand attitudes and purchase intentions both directly and indirectly, by enhancing audience acceptance of ad claims.

Contributor

Richard J. Lutz, University of Florida

References

Brown, Steven P., Pamela M. Homer, and J. Jeffrey Inman (1998), "A Meta-Analysis of Relationships Between Ad-Evoked Feelings and Advertising Responses." *Journal of Marketing Research* 35 (February), 114–26.

Brown, Steven P., and Douglas M. Stayman (1992), "Antecedents and Consequences of Attitude toward the Ad: A Meta-analysis." *Journal of Consumer Research* 19 (June), 34–51.

Haley, Russell I., and Allan L. Baldinger (2000), "The ARF Copy Research Validity Project." *Journal of Advertising Research* 40 (November), 114–35.

1. Correlation (r) is a measure of linear association between two variables, ranging between -1 and $+1$. The higher the correlation in absolute value, the more tightly the two variables co-move with each other. Correlation measures linear association but does not establish the direction of causality between the two variables.

Brand Effects

14

Consumer Brand Recall

Insights

Brand recall is the likelihood and speed with which a brand name comes to mind as a response to a marketplace cue (e.g., the product class name, a specific consumer need, etc.).[1] It is generally regarded as one of two aspects of brand awareness, the other being brand recognition (not covered here, brand recognition is the feeling of familiarity or knowledge consumers experience in response to a brand name, logo, or package). Brand awareness is regarded as an important component of brand equity (along with brand image and brand loyalty).

There are four robust empirical findings about brand recall:
- Brand recall is correlated with market shares in analyses of aggregate data and with consumer choice in analyses of individual-level data. Experimental studies that manipulate recall find that higher recall leads to higher choice shares, both immediately and after a delay. Inclusion in consumers' consideration sets is widely accepted as the causal mechanism underlying this effect.
- The determinants of brand recall include personal preference, advertising expenditures, market share, and being representative of the product class.
- Closely competing brands tend to be recalled at the same time in clusters that reflect subcategories in the larger product class. Anything that brings a subcategory to mind enhances brand recall for the members of that subcategory. However, early recall of or exposure to a target brand exerts an inhibitory effect on subsequent recall of close competitors (i.e., brands in the same subcategory).
- Consumers who are more knowledgeable about a product class are able to recall more brands and show a greater ability to categorize those brands in a variety of ways, as the situation demands.

Evidence Base

Compilation of over 30 academic papers. The evidence base is mostly experimental laboratory-based research, but also includes a number of field studies by marketing research and advertising firms.

Managerial Implications

- Maintaining high levels of brand recall through marketing communications (e.g., advertising, packaging, and point-of-purchase marketing) should maintain or increase market share. However, because brand recall is heavily influenced by prior use and pre-existing preferences, it is not a good measure of exposure to specific marketing communications.
- Memory errors are biased toward brands with high levels of brand recall. When in doubt, people unconsciously assume the brand they saw in an ad or in a store was the one that comes to mind most easily. This contributes to the frequently noted advertising-to-sales-ratio advantage enjoyed by large market share brands.
- High levels of brand recall and/or in-store brand presence will inhibit brand recall for close competitors, reducing their sales in addition to increasing sales for the target brand.
- Small market-share brands should benefit most from awareness-oriented marketing communications, especially niche brands for which marketing communications associate the brand name with its subcategory in the product class.
- Market pioneers enjoy a first-mover advantage in brand recall and consideration.
- Brand extensions benefit from the high brand recall of the parent brand insofar as building awareness in the new product class is easier and requires fewer marketing resources compared to building a new brand name. Moreover, brand recall for the parent brand is often strengthened by promotion of the extension.

Contributor

J. Wesley Hutchinson, University of Pennsylvania

References

Alba, Joseph W., and Amitava Chattopadhyay (1985), "The Effects of Context and Part-Category Cues on the Recall of Competing Brands." *Journal of Marketing Research* 22 (August), 340–9.

Hutchinson, J. Wesley, Kalyan Raman, and Murali Mantrala (1994), "Finding Choice Alternatives in Memory: Probability Models of Brand Name Recall." *Journal of Marketing Research* 31 (November), 441–61.

Keller, Kevin (2008), *Strategic Brand Management*. Upper Saddle River, N.J.: Pearson Prentice Hall.

Nedungadi, Prakash (1990), "Recall and Consumer Consideration Sets: Influencing Choice without Altering Brand Evaluations." *Journal of Consumer Research* 17 (3), 263–76.

1. In the advertising research literature, brand recall sometimes refers to correctly recalling the name of the brand that was promoted in a specific advertisement or other marketing communication. Empirical findings for this type of research are not covered here.

15

Perceptions of Brand Extensions

Insights

Successful brand extensions to a new product category occur when the parent brand is seen as having favorable associations and consumers perceive a high degree of fit between the parent brand and the extension category. Favorable parent-brand associations include high quality, likability, and trustworthiness perceptions, as well as unique brand-specific associations. High perceived fit between the parent brand and extension category can be achieved in a number of different ways such as: (1) overall similarity between the original brand and extension category, (2) technical or manufacturing commonalities, (3) complementarities in usage occasions or users, and (4) relevance of brand-specific associations in the extension category.

Additional factors that increase the likelihood of extension success are past consumer usage of the parent brand, marketing support that highlights the benefits of the brand extension, and wide retail distribution.

Evidence Base

Analysis of eight experimental data sets from the U.S., England, France, and Australia and survey of 2,400 German respondents regarding consumer packaged goods brand extensions, as well as a large number of controlled lab experiments.

Managerial Implications

Parent brand characteristics
- Numerous characteristics of a parent brand should be considered when evaluating its extension potential, including perceptions of quality, likability, and trustworthiness, as well as brand-specific associations and perceptions of brand breadth.
- A parent brand that consumers see as prototypical of a product category can be lim-

ited in extending outside its original category. In contrast, broad brands that offer products in diverse categories have an advantage in extending to distant categories.

Perceived fit

- Many additional factors can affect the perceived fit of the brand extension: product-related attributes and benefits, non-product-related attributes and benefits related to common usage situations, and manufacturing expertise.
- Extending to a category where brand-specific associations are relevant can be a more influential factor in extension success than high parent brand likability or overall similarity between product categories.
- Brands can more easily grow through a sequence of "little steps" and close-fitting extensions rather than attempting "big jumps" and largely dissimilar extensions.
- Consumer characteristics such as brand and category knowledge, processing style, and self-construal affect perceptions of fit. Consumers who are holistic (versus analytic) processors and possess interdependent (versus independent) self-construals perceive higher fit for distant extensions.

Extension characteristics

- Brand extension success is dependent on the competitive context with, for example, extending brands having greater success when they are relatively more familiar than existing brands in the extension category.
- Vertical extensions where the extension is lower or higher in price and quality than the parent brand can be difficult and often require sub-branding.

Marketing support

- Marketing support is important for extension success. The most effective advertising strategy for a brand extension is one that emphasizes information about the extension rather than the parent brand.

Contributors

Susan M. Broniarczyk, University of Texas at Austin, and Kevin Lane Keller, Dartmouth College

References

Bottomley, Paul A., and Stephen J. S. Holden (2001), "Do We Really Know How Consumers Evaluate Brand Extensions? Empirical Generalizations Based on Secondary Analysis of Eight Studies." *Journal of Marketing Research* 38 (November), 494–500.

Volckner, Franziska, and Henrik Sattler (2006), "Drivers of Brand Extension Success." *Journal of Marketing* 70 (April), 18–34.

16

Brand Dilution and Protection

Insights

Two conclusions emerge from the literature on brand dilution. One conclusion is that strong brands, which are familiar to consumers who have positive beliefs and experiences with the brand, are less likely to be diluted or harmed by negative publicity about a brand, by product harm crises and product recalls, by brand extension failures, and by trademark infringement of competing brands.

The second conclusion is that when brand extensions are inconsistent with a brand's image—because they are in product categories far away from the brand's typical offerings, have attributes or features not associated with the brand, or turn out to be failures—the parent brands can be diluted and harmed. However, these types of brand extensions pose less risk for brand dilution when:

- The brand extension is launched using a brand architecture option that distances the parent brand from the brand extension—for example, using a sub-brand or endorsed brand (e.g., Courtyard by Marriott).
- The brand extension is launched with the aid of a co-branding partner who provides a better fit for the extension category or the attributes/benefits important to the product. For example, Betty Crocker brownie mix with Hershey's chocolate syrup (co-branded extension for Hershey's) has a lower risk for brand dilution than a single-branded product (Hershey's brownie mix).

Evidence Base

Review of 25 years of empirical research published in major marketing journals; conclusions are based on more than 60 individual studies (in more than 35 journal articles), primarily experiments.

Managerial Implications

Building strong brands is usually viewed as a way to establish customer loyalty, build in price premiums, and increase sales. However, strong brands also provide insurance against unforeseen negative events that can harm brands.

Firms should take special care to reduce the risks of brand dilution when launching brand extensions that are inconsistent with the brand's image and product category expertise. The risks can be managed by using certain brand architecture options, such as sub-brands or endorsed brands or by taking on a co-brand partner to reduce the perceived inconsistency of the extension.

Contributors

Barbara Loken, University of Minnesota, and Deborah Roedder John, University of Minnesota

References

John, Deborah Roedder, and Barbara Loken (2010), "When Do Bad Things Happen to Good Brands? Understanding Internal and External Sources of Brand Dilution." Minneapolis, Minn.: Institute for Research in Marketing, Carlson School of Management, White paper.

Loken, Barbara, and Deborah Roedder John (2010), "When Do Bad Things Happen to Good Brands? Understanding Internal and External Sources of Brand Dilution." In *Brands and Brand Management: Contemporary Research Perspectives*, eds. Barbara Loken, Rohini Ahluwalia, and Michael J. Houston, 233–70. London, U.K.: Taylor & Francis.

Consumer Inferences

17

Consumer Inferences and Assumptions

Insights

Consumers frequently use easy-to-evaluate information (price, brand, appearance) to draw inferences about difficult-to-evaluate properties (missing attributes, quality, reliability).

People are typically insensitive to missing or unmentioned attributes, alternatives, or possibilities, and this leads to strong opinions on the basis of weak evidence. People make better inferences and decisions when they are sensitive to missing information, due to high knowledge or high motivation to process information analytically or comparatively.

Evidence Base

Reviews of over 190 academic articles, books, and book chapters. Evidence base is mainly laboratory based.

Managerial Implications

Because consumers use a wide variety of cues to infer quality, it is important to determine which cues are important in a given product category.

Because asking questions about inferences encourages consumers to form measurement-induced inferences that they might not form otherwise, it is important to use research techniques to assess spontaneous inference elicitation. Spontaneously formed inferences are more likely to generalize from the laboratory to the field, are easier to retrieve from memory, are held with greater confidence, and are more likely to influence other judgments and decisions.

Consumers hold so many assumptions about products that these assumptions often compete with one another and, in some cases, contradict one another. Consequently, consumers will draw different conclusions from the same information, depending on which assumption is salient at the time of judgment.

For example, high price can imply high quality or low value, depending on whether consumers focus on quality or value. Product popularity can imply high or low quality, depending on whether consumers focus on popularity appeals (one million satisfied customers cannot be wrong) or on scarcity appeals (rare products are valuable and desirable). Ads containing technical jargon can be either effective or ineffective, depending on whether consumers focus on ad informativeness or on ad comprehensibility.

Contributor
Frank R. Kardes, University of Cincinnati

References
Kardes, Frank R., Steven S. Posavac, and Maria L. Cronley (2004), "Consumer Inference: A Review of Processes, Bases, and Judgment Contexts." *Journal of Consumer Psychology* 14 (3), 230–56.

Kardes, Frank R., Steven S. Posavac, Maria L. Cronley, and Paul M. Herr (2008), "Consumer Inference." In *Handbook of Consumer Psychology*, eds. Curtis P. Haugtvedt, Paul M. Herr, and Frank R. Kardes, 165-91. New York, N.Y.: Lawrence Erlbaum Associates.

18

Perceptions of Quality Signals

Insights

Consumers use a variety of signals (i.e., costly actions by the firm) to infer the quality or price of a firm's products. Such signals reduce consumer uncertainty in situations in which they lack other information (e.g., new or unfamiliar products, new product categories, low consumer expertise).

Signals of high quality include brand names, high prices, high manufacturer warranties, brand alliances, retailer reputation, advertising expenditures, and product return policies. Brand names and price are the most commonly used signals, followed by manufacturer warranties. Signals of low product quality include price promotions and low price and price-matching guarantees.

Consumers infer quality from a signal when they think the signal is credible, i.e., the firm stands to lose money or reputation if it fails to deliver on the signal. Because of this, consumers perceive signals as more credible when offered by high-reputation firms than low-reputation firms. However, low-reputation firms can benefit from partnering with reputable retailers or brand allies.

Consumers notice the costliness of a signal when the cost is visible (e.g., Super Bowl advertising) or exceeds expectations. Further, consumers distrust signals that seem too good to be true, e.g., advertising spending that is significantly greater than that of competitors. In this case, signaling can backfire, as consumers may think the company does not have confidence in its quality.

Evidence Base

Compilation of 47 academic papers, reporting 80 empirical studies. Evidence is based on 15 analyses of secondary data, 4 analyses of survey data, and 61 laboratory experiments.

Managerial Implications

- Managers of high-quality products should make sure that consumers realize that they are incurring costly expenditures. This means making typically opaque costs, such as R&D or brand-building investments, visible to consumers.
- Managers should make sure that consumers don't perceive the expenditures as excessive, which would indicate low confidence in quality.
- Managers of new or unfamiliar brands should use well-known retailers or other reputable brand allies to reduce consumer uncertainty about product quality.
- Unknown sellers on the Internet can signal high product quality by setting a high reference price (i.e., starting bid price), and reduce consumers' uncertainty by building a strong reputation through positive buyer feedback.

Contributors

Amna Kirmani, University of Maryland, and James Kim, University of Maryland

References

Boulding, William, and Amna Kirmani (1993), "A Consumer Side Experimental Examination of Signaling Theory: Do Consumers Perceive Warranties as Signals of Quality?" *Journal of Consumer Research* 20 (1), 111–23.

Kirmani, Amna, and Akshay R. Rao (2000), "No Pain, No Gain: A Critical Review of the Literature on Signaling Unobservable Product Quality." *Journal of Marketing* 64 (April), 66–79.

Srivastava, Joydeep, and Nicholas Lurie (2001), "A Consumer Perspective on Price-Matching Refund Policies: Effect on Price Perceptions and Search Behavior." *Journal of Consumer Research* 28 (2), 296–307.

19

Causal Inferences and Consumers' Judgments

Insights

When people ask themselves *why* events occurred, such as why was service bad, why did a spokesperson endorse a product, and why is this product offered at a discount, their answers are often in the form of explanations or causal attributions (e.g., the product is discounted because no one wants it).

Different people can confidently arrive at different causal attributions for the same outcome. Differences are sometimes due to motivational factors (e.g., the need to think of oneself in the best possible light; the goal to identify an action to take) and sometimes due to the accessibility of information (e.g., consumers often lack the knowledge to understand how they might have misused a product). These differences are important because inferences about causes influence a person's other cognitions (e.g., who is blamed for product failure), emotional reactions (e.g., how angry the consumer feels about product failure), and actions (e.g., whether the consumer is willing to repurchase the product).

More specifically,
- Consumers are suspicious that marketers have ulterior motives. Marketing communications that belie those expectations, such as two-sided messages, can lead consumers to revise their inferences about the firm's intent and so are more persuasive.
- In the absence of the firm's offering a credible explanation for a price deal on a product, consumers generally infer reasons that reflect badly on the product's value. For this reason, a large purchase incentive undermines liking for the product more than when a firm gives a small incentive to purchase.
- Consumers value those who expend effort on their behalf and on others' behalf (e.g., service providers who work longer to make a product, employees who engage in charitable activities, firms who behave in a socially responsible manner). Resulting feelings of gratitude can lead to consumer actions that benefit the firm (e.g., recommending the firm to others).
- Consumers tend to assume that other consumers share their opinions about a product and to anticipate that other consumers will react similarly to a company's actions

(e.g., that others will be as attracted to a promotion as they are).

- Product failure is likely to prompt customers to think about causes for this outcome. People generally do not attribute really bad outcomes merely to bad luck. When a firm fails to offer an explanation, customers often infer that the firm is responsible and blame the firm, which leads to anger at the firm, less repurchase, increased complaints, and even desires to hurt the firm. Likelihood to repurchase improves if a firm gives an "account" or explanation for a problem that identifies a cause outside the firm's control and that is unlikely to persist.

Evidence Base

Over 300 articles, describing over 1,000 individual studies, mostly laboratory experiments with students as participants.

Managerial Implications

- Managers should explain the company's actions to customers: why a product failed, why a price deal or promotion is being offered, why a product is superior, and so forth. They should not assume that customers interpret the company's actions the same way they do.
- Managers should provide credible explanations that convey their good intentions, both through the content of a message and through the use of execution elements in marketing communications that support such inferences. They should let consumers know when employees have exerted effort to make a better product or to help customers.
- Describing an offering as scarce or limited in quantity will hasten purchase among those who already value the product. They will believe that others will compete for the product.
- Since large incentives can decrease liking for a product, managers should offer promotional incentives that are just sufficient to generate purchase.
- Managers should explain product problems—as well as reasons for offering a promotion—by pointing to causes that are temporary and will not be a factor in the future. Further, they should communicate explanations promptly, before consumers arrive at a different explanation.
- Managers should exercise caution in challenging a customer's explanation—even when the firm is not to blame for the problem. Rather than arguing with the customer over the "right" cause, the firm may be better off in the long term by not contesting the customer's explanation, expressing sympathy, and offering some remedy for product failure.

Contributor
Valerie S. Folkes, University of Southern California

References

Folkes, Valerie S. (1988), "Recent Attribution Research in Consumer Behavior: A Review and New Directions." *Journal of Consumer Research* 14 (March), 548–65.

Kardes, Frank R., Steven S. Posavac, Maria L. Cronley, and Paul M. Herr (2008), "Consumer Inference." In *Handbook of Consumer Psychology*, eds. Curtis P. Haugtvedt, Paul M. Herr, and Frank R. Kardes, 165–91. New York, N.Y.: Lawrence Erlbaum Associates.

Silvera, David H., and Daniel Laufer (2005), "Recent Developments in Attribution Research and Their Implications for Consumer Judgments and Behavior." In *Advertising and Consumer Psychology*, eds. Frank Kardes, Paul Herr, and Jacques Nantel, 53–77. Mahwah, N.J.: Erlbaum.

20

Consumer Use of Persuasion Knowledge

Insights

Consumers are smarter than we think. They have intuitive theories or beliefs about how marketers try to influence them, and under certain conditions, they use these beliefs to counter persuasion attempts. Consumers' persuasion knowledge includes beliefs about marketers' motives, persuasion tactics, appropriateness and effectiveness of different persuasion tactics, and strategies for coping with influence attempts.

Consumers' use of persuasion knowledge has been demonstrated in a large number of marketing contexts, including beliefs about the appropriateness and effectiveness of advertising tactics, product placement, and celebrity endorsers; the motives and tactics of salespeople; the motives underlying corporate social responsibility efforts; pricing and product bundling strategies; and word-of-mouth used in social media.

When persuasion knowledge is activated, consumers become suspicious of marketers' ulterior motives. This leads to resistance to persuasion and negative responses to the marketer.

Consumers are likely to use persuasion knowledge when the accessibility of firms' ulterior motives is high (e.g., because persuasion tactics are blatant, incongruent, or inappropriately used) and when consumers have high cognitive capacity, i.e., the time and ability to think about what the marketer is doing.

In the advertising and promotions context, suspicion of firms' motives may be raised by the use of rhetorical questions, puffery, negative ad comparisons, disclosures and fine print, borrowed interest appeal, incongruent placement of brands in television shows, advocacy advertising, and some types of cause-related marketing.

Suspicion of firms' motives may also be raised by a salesperson's use of flattery, some types of bargaining strategies, some types of cause-related marketing, partially comparative pricing, biased sources, visual packaging similarity, the disclosure of financial rewards to online bloggers, and expensive default options.

Because of years of experience with persuading and being persuaded, older adults have better-developed persuasion knowledge than young adults. However, the elderly are less likely to use persuasion knowledge because of their lower cognitive abilities.

Evidence Base

Compilation of 40 academic papers, reporting 91 empirical studies. Evidence is based on 85 laboratory experiments, 4 longitudinal surveys, and 2 interpretive studies.

Managerial Implications

1 The advent of the Internet and social media has made consumers more persuasion savvy than before. Consumers have more information about products and services as well as information about persuasion strategies. Managers who fail to recognize consumers' use of persuasion knowledge will lose customers.

2 In order to avoid resistance to persuasion, managers must understand the potential triggers of persuasion knowledge in their touch points with the consumer. In the context of your brand or category, what is likely to make consumers think, "They're trying to get me"?

3 Consumers are becoming more and more suspicious of online bloggers touting products. Thus, a blogger's attempt to tout a product may actually backfire and reduce consumer trust in both the blogger and the product.

Contributor
Amna Kirmani, University of Maryland

References

Campbell, Margaret, and Amna Kirmani (2000), "Consumers' Use of Persuasion Knowledge: The Effects of Accessibility and Cognitive Capacity on Perceptions of an Influence Agent." *Journal of Consumer Research* 27 (June), 69–83.

Campbell, Margaret, and Amna Kirmani (2008), "I Know What You're Doing and Why You're Doing It: The Use of the Persuasion Knowledge Model in Consumer Research." In *Handbook of Consumer Psychology*, eds. Curtis P. Haugtvedt, Paul M. Herr, and Frank R. Kardes, 549–74. New York, N.Y.: Lawrence Erlbaum Associates.

Friestad, Marian, and Peter Wright (1994), "The Persuasion Knowledge Model: How People Cope with Persuasion Attempts." *Journal of Consumer Research* 21 (June), 1–31.

Feelings, Attitudes, and Persuasion

21

Effects of Mere Exposure on Brand Liking

Insights

Mere exposure to a stimulus (e.g., a brand name), without any accompanying message or reinforcement, is sufficient to increase liking of that stimulus. Awareness of having been exposed to the stimulus is not necessary for the effect, and in fact inhibits it. In addition, effects are stronger for briefer, even subliminal, exposures. Effects are also stronger when the presented stimulus is intermixed with other stimuli and when there is a delay between the exposure and the attitude assessment, even if the delay is substantial (e.g., two weeks). Mere exposure increases liking primarily among adults, not children.

Evidence Base

Meta-analysis of 134 published articles; many articles published after the meta-analysis.

Managerial Implications

Brand managers cannot only increase "top-of-mind awareness" by repeatedly exposing consumers to their brand; they can also increase liking. Event promotions, product placements, and the like can increase liking even (or especially) among those unaware of their exposure to the brand, and these effects are likely to persist long after the exposure.

Contributor
S. Christian Wheeler, Stanford University

References

Bornstein, Robert F. (1989), "Exposure and Affect: Overview and Meta-Analysis of Research, 1968–1987." *Psychological Bulletin* 106 (2), 265–89.

Zajonc, Robert B. (1968), "Attitudinal Effects of Mere Exposure." *Journal of Personality and Social Psychology Monographs* 9 (2, pt. 2), 1–27.

22

The Influence of Feelings and Emotions on Consumers' Judgments

Insights

Consumers' emotional feelings toward products and services tend to exert strong influences on their evaluations of and preferences for these products and services. These influences can arise without the consumers realizing that their evaluations and judgments are actually driven by their emotional feelings. This is because emotional feelings tend to bias consumers' thoughts in the direction of their feelings, leaving consumers to inappropriately believe that their judgments were actually based on thinking rather than feelings.

These feeling effects arise even if the actual source of the feelings (e.g., an attractive salesperson) is not the product or service to which the consumer attributes those feelings. However, these effects tend to be more pronounced when consumers have experiential motives (e.g., choosing a hotel for a vacation) or when the product category is mostly hedonic (e.g., perfume) than when consumers have instrumental motives (e.g., choosing a hotel to host a business event) or when the product category is mostly utilitarian (e.g., a dishwasher).

Evidence Base

Compilation of more than 40 academic articles, reporting more than 100 empirical studies, mostly laboratory experiments with some correlational studies.

Managerial Implications

- Marketers should pay close attention to the emotional feelings, positive or negative, that consumers associate with their offerings.
- Marketers should not neglect sources of feelings that may seem incidental to the products or services, but are in fact attributed to these products and services.

- Marketers cannot expect to offset negative emotional feelings with positive factual information, but positive emotional feelings will tend to withstand negative factual information.

These recommendations hold across product categories and settings, although more so for hedonic and experiential categories and settings than for utilitarian and instrumental categories and settings.

Contributor
Michel Tuan Pham, Columbia University

References

Pham, Michel Tuan (1998), "Representativeness, Relevance, and the Use of Feelings in Decision Making." *Journal of Consumer Research* 25 (September), 144–59.

Pham, Michel Tuan (2007), "Emotion and Rationality: A Critical Review and Interpretation of Empirical Evidence." *Review of General Psychology* 11 (2), 155–78.

Pham, Michel Tuan, Joel B. Cohen, John Pracejus, and G. David Hughes (2001), "Affect Monitoring and the Primacy of Feelings in Judgment." *Journal of Consumer Research* 28 (September), 167–88.

23

Persuasion: Elaboration Likelihood Model

Insights

The study of persuasion considers how attitudes can be altered. While theorists have proposed multiple routes to persuasion, the most popular framework is the elaboration likelihood model (ELM). This model proposes two routes to persuasion: central and peripheral.

A consumer employing the *central route* is persuaded through cognitive processing of the merits of a product or service. An attitude is formed or altered as a result of the strength of the communicated arguments (e.g., an advertisement). For the central route to occur, the consumer has to be both able and motivated to process these arguments.

A consumer employing a *peripheral route* has low motivation and/or ability to process communicated arguments and is instead persuaded by peripheral cues in the message environment. Peripheral cues are not directly related to the product and do not serve as relevant arguments. In the case of advertising, these cues might include music, color, size of a print ad, celebrity status of the endorser, etc.

Two tenets of the ELM seem most critical to the marketing environment. First, a variable can serve multiple roles (e.g., a peripheral cue, a relevant product argument, a distractor that reduces processing), depending on the message environment. For example, an attractive advertising model may serve as a peripheral cue for an automobile and as an implied visual argument for a shampoo. Second, persuasion that occurs as a result of the central route—when consumers are focused on careful processing of the message arguments—results in far more strongly held attitudes that tend to persist over time and are more resistant to counterarguments.

Evidence Base

More than 400 research studies in advertising, communication, counseling, health, law, marketing, and personality and social psychology spanning 30 years.

Managerial Implications

The ELM provides significant food for thought with regard to marketing strategy. When a product is operating in a marketplace environment where consumer motivation is low, a focus on positively perceived peripheral cues that become associated with the product over time will likely be most helpful in altering attitudes (e.g., marketing to consumers in a highly competitive CPG environment).

Under conditions where consumers are highly motivated to process message arguments, the use of peripheral cues (e.g., attractive models, celebrities) will not be nearly as important as the quality of the message arguments provided (e.g., business-to-business marketing).

Contributor
David W. Schumann, University of Tennessee

References

Petty, Richard E., and John T. Cacioppo (1986), *Communication and Persuasion: Central and Peripheral Routes to Attitude Change.* New York, N.Y.: Springer/Verlag.

Petty, Richard E., John T. Cacioppo, and David Schumann (1983), "Central and Peripheral Routes to Advertising Effectiveness: The Moderating Role of Involvement." *Journal of Consumer Research* 10 (September), 135–46.

Petty, Richard E., and Pablo Briñol (in press), "The Elaboration Likelihood Model." In *Handbook of Theories of Social Psychology*, eds. P. A. M. Van Lange, A. Kruglanski, and E. T. Higgins. London, U.K.: Sage.

Schumann, David W., Michael R. Kotowski, Ho-Young (Anthony) Ahn, and Curtis P. Haugtvedt (forthcoming), "A Review of 30 Years of ELM Research in Advertising." In *Theoretical Perspectives in Advertising*, eds. S. Rogers and E. Thorson. London, U.K.: Routledge|Taylor and Francis Group.

24

Consumer Goal Orientation

Consumers are goal-driven. They are driven by their consumption goals as well as by some higher order orientation that governs the way they pursue their goals. This orientation that influences how people pursue their goals is known as "regulatory focus."

Those with a *promotion focus* orient their attention, attitudes, and behaviors toward achieving their ideals and aspirations. They think more abstractly, look further ahead into the future, and are motivated by positive outcomes; these individuals pursue their goals with eagerness and are concerned about missed opportunities. In contrast, those with a *prevention focus* are driven to fulfill their responsibilities and obligations. They think more concretely, pay attention to their immediate environment, and are motivated to avoid negative outcomes; these individuals pursue their goals with vigilance and are more concerned about taking the wrong step.

People may adopt a promotion or prevention focus because of their disposition or cultural background (people from a Western culture tend to be promotion-focused, whereas those from an Eastern culture tend to be prevention-focused) or in response to a particular situation at hand.

People are more persuaded by messages that match their regulatory focus, especially when they are not motivated to process information. For example, promotion-focused individuals are more persuaded by messages that emphasize hopes and ideals, gains and non-gains, growth and accomplishments, and *why* one should do certain things; whereas prevention-focused individuals are more persuaded by messages that highlight duties and obligations, losses and non-losses, safety and security, and *how* one should do things.

People who approach their goal in a manner that fits with their focus (i.e., eager strategies for the promotion-focused and vigilant strategies for the prevention-focused) are also more engaged and have better self-control than those who employ strategies that do not fit with their focus.

Evidence Base

More than 150 academic articles, each with 2–5 studies examining the effects of regulatory focus on judgment, choice, and self-regulation. Most evidence is laboratory based, with some involving actual behaviors.

Managerial Implications

Managers should develop messages that match the regulatory focus of the target audience and ensure consistency within a message. For example, an appeal for fruit juice could explain why vitamin C has energizing benefits when targeting young consumers, who are likely to be promotion-focused, or describe how antioxidants can unclog arteries when targeting elderly consumers, who tend to be prevention-oriented. And an effective message for financial services could highlight growth opportunities and long-term gains (but not short-term gains), or it could emphasize hedging opportunities to avoid immediate losses (but not downstream losses).

Sometimes the brand or product category may prompt the target audience to adopt a particular regulatory focus (e.g., buyers of home security systems or insecticides may adopt a prevention focus, and car buyers going on a test drive in a BMW may adopt a promotion focus). And it pays for managers to find out whether their brand has a promotion or prevention appeal when developing their positioning strategy.

Contributor

Angela Y. Lee, Northwestern University

References

Higgins, E. T. (2000), "Making a Good Decision: Value from Fit." *American Psychologist* 55 (11), 1217–30.

Lee, Angela Y., and E. Tory Higgins (2009), "The Persuasive Power of Regulatory Fit." In *The Social Psychology of Consumer Behavior*, ed. Michaela Wänke, 319–33. New York, N.Y.: Psychology Press.

25

Consumer Attitudes Toward Marketing

Insights

Based on longitudinal national poll results, the Notre Dame–Socratic Technologies Index of Consumer Sentiment toward Marketing (ICSM) score, the general attitude of American consumers regarding marketing practice has improved over the decades. It has risen from –14.9 in 1983 to +4.24 in 2010 (on a scale of –200 to +200). The cited raw scores translate into an improvement in index numbers from 100 to 105.62. This trend, which is significant, is mainly due to secular increases in the product- and price-oriented components of the sentiment measure.

Evidence Base

33,365 panel responses to a validated 24-item scale instrument, from (nearly) annual data collection over the 1983–2010 period (hiatus in 2007–08), representing the U.S. consumer household market. Data collection conducted via the Synovate (formerly Market Facts) Consumer Mail Panel through 2006, by Socratic Technologies since 2009.

Managerial Implications

Public sentiment toward the institution of marketing in the U.S. is improving, long term, and appears to be relatively neutral, not hostile. More specifically:

- Product and price, among the basic marketing mix elements, appear to contribute more to general consumer sentiment (the ICSM) than distribution/retailing and advertising do. However, concerning the absolute level of component sentiment scores, distribution/retail and product are now viewed more favorably than advertising and price, perhaps not surprisingly. (In earlier years of the study, sentiment toward product actually had been more negative than that toward advertising.)
- Demographics are found to have very little relation to general consumer attitude toward marketing, but some macroeconomic variables do relate. The inflation and na-

tional saving rates both seem to depress consumer sentiment toward marketing, apparently by reducing consumption utility. The ICSM also relates inversely to the U.S. crime rate as a dependent variable!

Contributor
John F. Gaski, University of Notre Dame

References
Gaski, John F., and Michael J. Etzel (1986), "The Index of Consumer Sentiment Toward Marketing." *Journal of Marketing* 50 (3), 71–81.

Gaski, John F., and Michael J. Etzel (2005), "National Aggregate Consumer Sentiment toward Marketing: A Thirty-Year Retrospective and Analysis." *Journal of Consumer Research* 31 (4), 859–67.

Gaski, John F. (2008), "The Index of Consumer Sentiment toward Marketing: Validation, Updated Results, and Demographic Analysis." *Journal of Consumer Policy* 31 (2), 195–216.

Decision Making and Purchase

26

Pre-choice Bias in Brand Choice

Insights

For many years, researchers believed that consumers making a brand decision without a habitual preference would not bias how they viewed product information until after a brand had been chosen. How could they bias to support a preferred brand when they didn't yet know which brand they preferred?

What research has revealed is that consumers can bias *toward an emerging preference*, that is, toward whichever product is leading in overall preference at any time during the purchase decision. A series of studies has consistently found that consumers bias their evaluation of new product information to be too supportive of whichever brand is currently leading in their preference. The greater the tentative preference, the greater is the bias in the consumer evaluation of the next piece of product information. In one study, consumers chose an inferior product over half the time as long as the single most positive attribute for that inferior brand was shown first.

If a consumer sees information that causes a switch to another brand, the bias also switches to favor this new leading brand, just as if it had been leading all along. Consumers are totally unaware of their bias, which is almost impossible to eliminate. Since consumers can't detect the bias, they won't take advantage of even an explicit warning, and cash payments for accuracy only increase the bias (because the monetary incentive elevates consumers' mood, which, in turn, increases the bias).

The same advantage of being the initial leader in a consumer choice offers one explanation for how advertising influences brand choice. That is, consumers will choose a product based on superior advertising, even when they think the reason for their choice is subsequent product information.

Evidence Base

Dozens of studies over 15 years conducted in different contexts and by different researchers.

Managerial Implications

- A habitual preference for a brand provides a continuing advantage, even against a new product that may be superior. If consumers start a choice process with their habitual brand as their initial leader in preference, subsequent information is likely to be biased toward supporting that habitual choice.
- In order to establish an emerging preference, managers should try to control the order in which consumers consider product information, for example, positioning whatever is most positive about their brand as the first information that consumers see.

Contributor

J. Edward Russo, Cornell University

References

Meloy, Margaret G., J. Edward Russo, and Elizabeth G. Miller (2006), "Monetary Incentives and Mood." *Journal of Marketing Research* 43 (2), 267–75.

Russo, J. Edward, Kurt A. Carlson, and Margaret G. Meloy (2006), "Choosing an Inferior Option." *Psychological Science* 17 (October), 899–904.

Russo, J. Edward, and Anne-Sophie Chaxel (2010), "How Persuasive Messages Can Influence Behavior without Awareness." *Journal of Consumer Psychology* 20 (July), 338–42.

Russo, J. E., Margaret G. Meloy, and Victoria H. Medvec (1998), "Predecisional Distortion of Product Information." *Journal of Marketing Research* 35 (November), 438–52.

27

Consumers' Intertemporal Preferences

Intertemporal decisions, which involve trading off costs and benefits that are distributed over time, are ubiquitous and have been extensively studied in economics, psychology, and marketing. Common examples of intertemporal decisions include the decision to consume more today (i.e., borrow more and/or save less) in exchange for having less in your retirement fund; to purchase a cheaper refrigerator or AC unit, but forgo the ongoing energy savings; or to hire an average experienced employee who can start contributing immediately instead of a brilliant but inexperienced recent graduate who needs weeks of training.

Much of this research has compared actual behavior across different contexts to the normative standard—the discounted utility model, which assumes that the discounting rate of the utility is constant over time—and has demonstrated numerous violations of this normative model. More recently, research has shifted from identification of "anomalies" to uncovering the psychological determinants of intertemporal preferences. While there is a great deal of heterogeneity in individuals' discounting, the literature has uncovered several empirical generalizations.

Some key findings are:
- Consumers often heavily discount the future and focus on immediate costs and benefits (often referred to as "hyperbolic discounting"). This is manifested as (1) higher overall levels of discounting and (2) discount rates that are highly dependent on the time interval in question.
- The rate at which consumers discount the future is highly context dependent; for example, discounting is higher for smaller amounts than larger amounts, higher for gains than for losses, higher when delaying a current amount than when expediting a future amount, and often different for different resources (higher for time than money). There is only mixed evidence, at best, for the stability of discounting over situations.
- Consumers prefer improving sequences and strong endings (e.g., employees are hap-

pier with improving wage profiles, and consumers are happier with service that ends on a high note).

- Several key factors that drive intertemporal preferences are: (1) emotional reactions to immediate outcomes; (2) the mental representation of outcomes, with concrete evaluations of the near future and abstract evaluations of future outcomes; (3) the perception of different amounts of slack in a given resource (e.g., time, money) at different points in time; and (4) the perception of future time, including sensitivity to changes and subjective assessments of durations.

Evidence Base

More than 40 academic papers, including 2 review articles, reporting over 100 empirical studies. It is mostly laboratory based, with both real and hypothetical outcomes, and varies by insight (ranging from 2 to 25+ studies).

Managerial Implications

- Managers should consider the timing of costs and benefits to consumers. Higher adoption is more likely to occur when benefits are immediate and costs are deferred.
- Managers should be wary of consumers' stated intentions to take on future costs (such as upgrading or completing a survey).
- Managers should consider how an intertemporal decision is framed. For example, deferring current utility (receipt of a DVD) to a future date will result in steeper discounting than expediting future utility to the present.
- Managers should make future benefits concrete.
- When an experience or an interaction with the firm occurs over time, managers should try to provide an improving trend and end on a high note.

Contributor
Gal Zauberman, University of Pennsylvania

References
Frederick, Shane, George Loewenstein, and Ted O'Donoghue (2002), "Time Discounting and Time Preference: A Critical Review." *Journal of Economic Literature* 40 (2), 351–401.

Zauberman, Gal, and John G. Lynch (2005), "Resource Slack and Propensity to Discount Delayed Investments of Time versus Money." *Journal of Experiment Psychology: General* 134, 23–37.

Zauberman, Gal, B. Kyu Kim, Selin Malkoc, and James R. Bettman (2009), "Time Discounting and Discounting Time." *Journal of Marketing Research* 46 (August), 543–56.

28

Loss Aversion and Consumer Choice

Insights

Consumers tend to evaluate choice options in terms of changes relative to a reference point. Changes seen as losses tend to be evaluated more extremely than equivalent changes seen as gains. Typically, the pain of a loss is assessed to be roughly twice as intense as the pleasure of a comparable gain.

This asymmetry, known as loss aversion, contributes to a bias in favor of options seen as status quo or default options, compared to options that entail a mix of gains and losses. The perceived disadvantages of non-default alternatives tend to outweigh the perceived advantages and discourage their selection.

Another consequence of loss aversion is the endowment effect, a tendency to increase the valuation of a good when it is in one's possession. Owners tend to set their reservation prices higher than non-owners, because losing the good is imagined as more undesirable than acquiring the good is desirable. Similarly, owners of a good tend to show reluctance to trade it for another good, indicating a greater preference for the owned good than would be shown in a neutral choice between the two goods from the perspective of a non-owner.

Loss aversion also implies asymmetric responses to changes in marketing variables. Consumers are more sensitive to price increases or quality decreases than to equivalent price decreases or quality increases. When customizing products, consumers tend to prefer more features when removing features from a loaded model rather than adding features to a basic model.

Evidence Base

Compilation of 31 academic papers, including over 70 studies. Most studies involve hypothetical or small-stakes real choices, but effects are also found in field studies with substantial stakes.

Managerial Implications

- Marketing actions that induce temporary or perceived ownership (e.g., trial offers, free samples) will encourage longer-term acquisition of a good. Consumers will be willing to spend more to avoid losing a product than to acquire it initially.
- Product benefits framed as avoiding or removing losses may be more compelling to consumers than benefits framed as gains.
- Managers should strive to have their products perceived by consumers as status quo or default options.
- Managers should minimize the perceived disadvantages associated with a product, even at the expense of de-emphasizing other advantages. It may be preferable to frame an option as having one advantage and no disadvantages compared to competition, rather than four advantages and two disadvantages.
- Managers should expect and plan for exaggerated reaction to perceived losses when interpreting results of marketing research. Measured price elasticity in response to a price increase may be an overestimate of elasticity in response to a price decrease. Subjective valuations of products will depend on framing and the perspective of the respondent.

Contributor
Lyle Brenner, University of Florida

References
Hardie, Bruce, Eric Johnson, and Peter Fader (1993), "Modeling Loss Aversion and Reference Dependence Effects on Brand Choice." *Marketing Science* 12 (Fall), 378–94.

Kahneman, Daniel, Jack L. Knetsch, and Richard H. Thaler (1991), "The Endowment Effect, Loss Aversion, and Status Quo Bias." *Journal of Economic Perspectives* 5 (Winter), 19–206.

Novemsky, Nathan, and Daniel Kahneman (2005), "The Boundaries of Loss Aversion." *Journal of Marketing Research* 42 (May), 119–28.

29
Protected Values

Protected values are moral values that people believe should be exempt from the possibility of trading off. In the marketplace, protected values play a part in consumer responses when consumers feel that certain moral values (e.g., preserving the environment, protecting human rights) should not be sacrificed for price or non-moral quality attributes. For example, most people would not buy a product made from endangered baby animals, no matter how cheap or well-made. Protected values can exert a strong effect on market behavior, because they induce emotions such as sadness and anger, and because they embody consumers' strongly held moral values. In fact, the holding of protected values in the marketplace appears to be a way for consumers to help ensure that they adhere to their own moral rules.

Protected values lead to two types of market behavior, both in actual purchasing and in market research:

1 Consumers (irrationally) avoid information that may be relevant to protected values, in order to remain "willfully ignorant" and avoid the distress of having to react to the information.

2 Consumers inconsistently express their protected values across different purchasing contexts.

Willful Ignorance
Consumers who hold especially strong protected values may actually avoid finding out about attributes relevant to those protected values. For example, consumers who are passionate about rainforest preservation may nevertheless choose to remain ignorant of whether a piece of furniture is made with endangered rainforest wood or not. If they are given the information, however, they will use it in their decision making, reflecting their protected values in their purchasing.

Context Effects
1 Consumers are more likely to exhibit protected values when they are considering losing something than when they are considering gaining something. Thus, a pricing

task phrased as a selling task (e.g., "what is the least we could give you to sell this item?") will result in more refusals to respond than will a pricing task phrased in terms of buying (e.g., "what is the most you would pay to buy this item?"), because selling places more emphasis on loss than does buying.

Likewise, a product-winnowing task to exclude items from further consideration (i.e., "choose the products you do not wish to consider further") will result in more expression of protected values than will a product-winnowing task to include items for further consideration (i.e., "choose the products you wish to consider further"), because the former emphasizes the loss of goods from the consideration set.

2 Similarly, consumers are considerably more likely to exhibit protected values for actions (e.g., the company itself cut down a rainforest) than for inactions (e.g., the company did not stop locals from cutting down a rainforest, even though it had the power to do so).

Consumers are more likely to exhibit protected values when the task is more qualitative, such as choosing between two products or rating the attractiveness of products on an arbitrary scale, than when it is more quantitative, such as providing a buying price for the item. Conversely, sometimes the mere mention of money in relation to particularly sacred items, such as religious items, can result in a strong exhibition of protected values, including considerable negative emotion.

Protected values appear to differ by context for two reasons. First, different contexts provide stronger or weaker activation of moral rules. For example, excluding items appears to be more compatible with moral reasoning, because most moral rules involve "thou shall not" admonitions of what should be rejected. Second, different contexts highlight different aspects of the decision. In a pricing task, people are paying attention to the cost of the item and the effect of the item on their wallets. In a choice task, people may be thinking more holistically, as if they were voting for the item or choosing to support it as in a charity. Indeed, political and philanthropic contexts seem to encourage more expression of protected values than do some market contexts.

Evidence Base

Approximately 15 peer-reviewed journal articles, as well as a number of book chapters providing overviews of relevant research.

Managerial Implications

For managers of products with attributes that are positive in ways that might be relevant to some consumers' protected values (e.g., that are environmentally friendly, made without child labor, do not exploit local economies, etc.), several strategies might help ensure that consumers express their moral values in support of the deserving product:

1 Because willful ignorance is prevalent in the target segment, managers should provide easy-to-understand information about the moral attribute in marketing communications and at point-of-purchase.

2 Managers should encourage consumers to think of the decision in terms of losses and exclusions. For example, advertising could tell consumers "do not leave us out!" or "think about all you would lose without us!"

3 Managers should encourage consumers away from focusing on price, by framing the decision in terms of voting, for example, or in terms of choice. Advertising, point-of-purchase, and labeling can all encourage contexts that cue protected values.

Contributor
Julie Irwin, University of Texas

References
Baron, Jon, and Mark Spranca (1997), "Protected Values." *Organizational Behavior and Human Decision Processes* 70 (April), 1–16.

Ehrich, Kristine, and Julie R. Irwin (2005), "Willful Ignorance: The Avoidance of Ethical Attribute Information." *Journal of Marketing Research* 42 (3), 266–77.

Irwin, Julie R., and Jonathan Baron (2001), "Response Mode Effects and Moral Values." *Organizational Behavior and Human Decision Processes* 84 (March), 177–97.

30

Purchase Intentions and Purchasing

Insights

Stated purchase intentions are strong, but imperfect, predictors of purchasing. On average, intentions are positively correlated with purchasing (average frequency weighted $r = 0.53$ in one study that looked at a wide range of general behaviors and 0.49 in another that focused on purchase-related behaviors).[1] However, the magnitude of the correlation varies considerably (in the first study the correlations ranged from 0.15 to 0.92; in the second they ranged from -0.13 to 0.99).

Many factors affect the strength of the relationship between purchase intentions and purchasing. Stated purchase intentions are more predictive of actual purchasing behavior (1) for existing products rather than new ones, (2) for durable goods rather than non-durable goods, (3) for short rather than long time horizons, and (4) for specific brands or models rather than products at the category level. Because of this, there is no one best way to weight intentions to forecast sales.

Evidence Base

One meta-analysis of data from 31 academic articles; a second meta-analysis of data from 21 academic articles and from 12 large-scale industry data sets.

Managerial Implications

Managers should measure intentions to help forecast future sales, but should be cautious when using intentions data. Managers should be aware that intentions are imperfect measures that in some cases are not related to future sales.

Contributor
Vicki G. Morwitz, New York University

References

Jamieson, Linda F., and Frank M. Bass (1989), "Adjusting Stated Purchase Intention Measures to Predict Trial Purchase of New Products: A Comparison of Models and Methods." *Journal of Marketing Research* 26 (August), 336–45.

Morwitz, Vicki G., Joel Steckel, and Alok Gupta (2007), "When Do Purchase Intentions Predict Sales?" *International Journal of Forecasting* 23 (3), 347–64.

Sheppard, Blair H., Jon Hartwick, and Paul R. Warshaw (1988), "The Theory of Reasoned Action: A Meta-Analysis of Past Research with Recommendations for Modifications and Future Research." *Journal of Consumer Research* 15 (3), 325–43.

1. Correlation (r) is a measure of linear association between two variables, ranging between -1 and $+1$. The higher the correlation in absolute value, the more tightly the two variables co-move with each other. Correlation measures linear association but does not establish the direction of causality between the two variables.

31

Consumer Habits and Purchase Behavior

Insights

Habits are dispositions to repeat a specific response that are learned through experience. They are cognitively represented as implicit associations between context cues (e.g., gym workout) and responses (e.g., drink Gatorade). Therefore, once habits form, perception of the cue automatically activates thought of the habitual response. Consumers form habits when they repeatedly purchase or consume items in a recurring context. Habits keep consumers repeating past behavior without necessarily considering the pros and cons of their actions. Consequently, because habits are triggered automatically by contexts, they hinder attempts at behavior change.

Implications for consumer behavior:
- Once habits are formed, consumers may repeatedly purchase and consume the same option triggered by context cues.
- When people have strong habits, advertising and new product information may change consumers' intentions but not carry over to changing their behavior.
- Changing habits requires conscious, effortful control. In order to inhibit the activated response in memory, consumers with strong habits must have sufficient motivation and ability to inhibit the habitual option and choose a new one.
- Consumer habits can be disrupted by altering the contextual cues that activate the habitual response.

Evidence Base

Two meta-analyses, one of 47 experiments and another of 60 experiments.

Managerial Implications

- Habitually loyal customers may have formed purchase and consumption habits without holding a corresponding preference. For these consumers, marketing efforts should be directed at changing behaviors—by changing existing habits and forming new ones.

- Marketing efforts should bolster stable performance contexts that induce a habitual response (e.g., fast-food logos that trigger purchase). Managers should design and structure loyalty programs so as to minimize changes in purchase and consumption contexts and thus to maintain habitually loyal customers.
- Everyday purchases can be changed more effectively through new homeowner marketing programs, such as Welcome Wagon. That is, consumers are especially receptive to such marketing when their habits are disrupted by new life contexts, such as relocation, taking a new job, or changing family status.

Contributors
Wendy Wood, University of Southern California, and Ravi Dhar, Yale University

References

Verplanken, Bas, and Wendy Wood (2006), "Interventions to Break and Create Consumer Habits." *Journal of Public Policy & Marketing* 25 (Spring), 90–103.

Wood, Wendy, and David T. Neal (2009), "The Habitual Consumer." *Journal of Consumer Psychology* 19 (October), 579–92.

32

Impulsive and Compulsive Buying

Impulsive and compulsive buying can both be seen as failures in self-regulation, yet they are distinctly different behaviors. Impulse buying often occurs because of a temporary depletion of a limited resource (cognitive, emotional, attentional, etc.) needed for self-regulation. Almost everyone engages in impulse buying from time to time, but 38% of adults classify themselves as impulse buyers.

Impulse buying is most likely to occur, and the amount spent is greater, immediately after people have expended cognitive, emotional, or attentional resources. It occurs more commonly when people are in positive mood states. Finally, impulse buying is greater when consumers think of themselves as being deprived by not having the good rather than simply wanting it.

Compulsive buying is a chronic failure of self-regulation, where the individual gives up self-control of purchasing in order to achieve a more primary need to temporarily alleviate negative self-feelings. It is a psychiatric disorder in which people experience an uncontrollable urge to buy, typically brought on by extreme negative self-feelings. It is estimated that between 5% and 6% of adults in the U.S. suffer from compulsive buying disorder.

Compulsive buyers frequently never use the things they purchase, and many eventually experience severe financial and personal problems as a result of this disorder.

Evidence Base

Compilation of 63 academic papers, reporting over 76 studies, that use a range of different methods, including surveys, laboratory experiments, field studies, and qualitative and psychiatric interviews.

Managerial Implications

Managers should be aware that impulse buying is more likely at the end of a shopping trip or after a busy day. Promotional strategies that enhance feelings of giving up a chance to have an item, such as through physical proximity (consumer trial) or temporal proximity (limited time offers), increase the likelihood of impulse buying.

Buying situations and venues that promote positive moods such as vacation resorts, locations featuring experiential activities such as theme parks, concerts, or stores offering activities (games or trial situations) or entertainment (videos or music) for consumers, or marketing on websites featuring games or entertainment activities may increase impulse purchase behavior.

Managers should be aware that compulsive buying behavior may appear similar to that of frequent or heavy consumers.

Contributors

Ronald J. Faber, University of Minnesota, and Kathleen D. Vohs, University of Minnesota

References

Faber, Ronald J., and Kathleen D. Vohs (2011), "Self-regulation and Spending: Evidence from Impulsive and Compulsive Buying." In *Handbook of Self-Regulation: Research, Theory and Applications*, 2nd ed., eds. Kathleen D. Vohs and R. F. Baumeister, 537–50. New York, N.Y.: Guilford Press.

Hoch, Stephen J., and George F. Loewenstein (1991), "Time Inconsistent Preferences and Consumer Self-control." *Journal of Consumer Research* 18 (March), 492–507.

Vohs, Kathleen D., and Ronald J. Faber (2007), "Spent Resources: Self-Regulatory Resource Availability Affects Impulse Buying." *Journal of Consumer Research* 33 (March), 537–47.

The Social Consumer

33

Social Contagion and Word-of-mouth

Insights

Attitudes and behaviors can spread contagiously to one's social connections. If a consumer purchases a product, engages in a consumption behavior, or adopts a new innovation, their friends, family members, co-workers, and other social connections will all be more likely to behave similarly. This social influence can occur actively or passively. Consumers actively sharing information through word-of-mouth, posting a link on social media websites, or writing an online review can change others' behavior. Consumers are also influenced by merely observing the behaviors of others, even if no communication takes place. Similar to the way in which a disease or virus spreads through a population, social ties provide a pathway through which information and influence can diffuse through social networks.

Evidence Base

Compilation of over 20 academic papers. Evidence is based mostly on archival data analysis and field experiments.

Managerial Implications

Companies should encourage word-of-mouth, both online and off. They should also make it easier for consumers to share information about their consumption behavior. This might include facilitating the distribution of brand-related content and behaviors on social media websites (e.g., badges on Facebook or social sharing buttons). Finally, they should try to make consumption more visible. This might include increasing logo sizes or generating public signals for private information (like the Intel Inside sticker on the outside of computers). The easier it is for people to see what others are doing, the more likely they will be to imitate them.

Contributor

Jonah Berger, University of Pennsylvania

References

Chevalier, Judith, and Dina Mayzlin (2006), "The Effect of Word of Mouth on Sales: Online Book Reviews." *Journal of Marketing Research* 43 (3), 345–54.

Godes, David, and Dina Mayzlin (2009), "Firm-Created Word-of-Mouth Communication: Evidence from a Field Study." *Marketing Science* 28 (4), 721–39.

Iyengar, Raghuram, Christophe Van den Bulte, and Thomas W. Valente (2011), "Opinion Leadership and Social Contagion in New Product Diffusion." *Marketing Science* 30 (2), 195–212.

34

Consumer Identity and Purchase Behavior

Insights

Consumers possess and can adopt a variety of identities (demographic, psychographic, and behavior-based), and these identities positively (negatively) influence attitudes and purchase intentions for products that align (misalign) with those identities. The influence of consumer identity on product evaluation generally depends on the momentary salience of the identity (how much the consumer is temporarily thinking about the identity) and how relevant the identity is at the moment a consumer judgment is called for.

To summarize:
- Consumers have multiple identities that are highly flexible across time and situations. Some identities within a consumer facilitate each other, while others may conflict. Consumers consciously and unconsciously balance the identities they strive for.
- Momentary activation of an identity increases when a consumer is "distinctive" in their social environment (usually because they are in the numeric minority) or when a consumer is exposed to images, exemplars, and other symbols in the media that direct attention to the identity.
- Consumers are generally more receptive to products that are associated with an activated identity—even when the consumer is unaware that the identity has been activated. Although consumers will also avoid products that are associated with identities that oppose their activated identity, receptivity to products associated with one's identity is generally more robust than the avoidance of products associated with opposing identities.
- Consumers will perceive the functional attributes of products associated with their identity as superior to other brands, even when they are objectively not.
- Consumers who choose products aligned with an identity often report subsequently more positive attitudes toward both the identity and themselves (self-esteem). Further, they will starkly defend brands that are aligned with their identity as if they were defending themselves.

Evidence Base

Compilation of 83 academic papers, reporting over 200 empirical studies. Evidence base includes both laboratory-based experiments and field studies.

Managerial Implications

- Marketers cannot assume that a consumer will always have a given identity "active," especially across different consumption contexts.
- Managers should incorporate identities into their promotions to the extent that the identities "fit" well with their brand's values, associations, and equity.
- There are often trade-offs between consumer identities such that targeting one identity may conflict with other identities the consumer possesses. Managers should therefore consider how their products and appeals may heighten or lessen internal conflict.
- Managers should incorporate imagery into their advertising that evokes the identity that the product is intended to activate.
- Managers should use social media and other promotions to connect a product to relevant consumer identities.
- Managers should reinforce identity linkages by producing complementary constellations of products that consumers can use to signal their identities to others. For example, an athletic brand is wise to produce general-purpose clothing that prominently displays its brand name and imagery, as this allows its consumers to signal that they are avid fans of the sport.
- Managers should routinely and carefully monitor and reassess the identity chosen and its ongoing linkages, to ensure that it remains authentic, relevant, timely, and distinct from competitor offerings.

Contributors

Mark R. Forehand, University of Washington, and Americus Reed II, University of Pennsylvania

References

Angle, Justin W., Mark R. Forehand, and Americus Reed II (forthcoming), "When Does Identity Salience Prime Approach and Avoidance: A Balance Congruity Model." In *Identity and Consumption*, eds. Ayalla Ruvio and Russell Belk. London, U.K.: Routledge/Taylor & Francis Group.

Forehand, Mark R., Andrew Perkins, and Americus Reed II (2011), "When Are Automatic Social Comparisons Not Automatic? The Effect of Cognitive Systems on User Imagery-based Self-concept Activation." *Journal of Consumer Psychology* 21(1), 88–100.

Forehand, Mark R., Rohit Deshpandé, and Americus Reed II (2002), "Identity Salience and the Influence of Differential Activation of the Social Self-schema on Advertising Response." *Journal of Applied Psychology* 87 (6), 1086–99.

Reed II, Americus (2004), "Activating the Self-Importance of Consumer Selves: Exploring Identity Salience Effects on Judgments." *Journal of Consumer Research* 31 (2), 286–95.

35

Perceptions of Advisors

Consumers frequently rely on one another to act as agents or advisors. Yet, consumers are selective about who they rely on and about the information they provide to others, in part based on their beliefs about others' knowledge, abilities, preferences, and intentions. Consumers do not always rely on those with the most expertise for information and advice. For example, for aesthetically evaluated products, consumers tend to seek out similar others. For functional products, consumers tend to seek out experts.

Preferences

When a consumer seeks an advisor with similar preferences, liking the same things, compared to disliking the same things, is more influential in evaluating similarity. When a consumer likes a product that a target individual likes, he or she will be likely to judge it as more informative about the target's underlying preferences than if the consumer dislikes a product that the target also dislikes.

When predicting others' preferences and others' knowledge, consumers overestimate the extent to which others will share their own preferences and knowledge, with greater overestimation for products they like than for products they dislike.

Consumers are more likely to rely on close friends whom they believe understand their preferences, but consumers overestimate the extent to which their close friends truly know them. So they may over-rely on friends' advice.

If consumers receive and attend to feedback about others' preferences, they may learn others' preferences, which may reduce overestimation of similarity and prediction error. However, this may be difficult in close relationships, because consumers, who think they know close others, may fail to pay attention to others' actual preferences or may be motivated to think preferences are more similar than they actually are.

Knowledge

An advisor's ability to recommend one good product, or the best product, from a set of many may differ from their ability to evaluate one specific product. The information a consumer needs to judge an advisor's probability of providing a successful recommendation versus a successful evaluation also differs. Consumers may confuse the information requirements for recommendations versus evaluations, so they may choose inferior advisors.

Consumers tend to misestimate their own knowledge and abilities relative to others, overestimating for topics and skills they find easy and underestimating for topics and skills that they find difficult. So they may not request help from others when they need it, and they may falsely believe they can provide help to others when they may not have the knowledge or skills to do so.

Advisors may try to manage others' beliefs about their own knowledge and intelligence. So they may not offer their true preferences, and instead may provide more negative evaluations in order to appear more knowledgeable, intelligent, or competent.

Trust and persuasiveness

Consumers may be reluctant to disclose sensitive or intimate information to an advisor, but they may be more willing to do so if the agent discloses similar information first, and if the disclosure moves from less to more intimate information.

Consumers may discount professional advisors as they try to protect themselves from what they see as attempts to persuade. However, if consumers are distracted, or are otherwise cognitively engaged, they may be disarmed and more likely to accept an advisor's advice.

When an advisor provides information that a consumer has requested, it may be judged as more valuable if it is provided more rapidly and in greater amounts and if the advisor engages in more frequent dialogue with the consumer.

Non-expert advisors may be more persuasive when they express an opinion with certainty, but experts may be more persuasive when they express less certainty in their claims.

Evidence Base

Compilation of 23 academic papers, each reporting multiple empirical studies. Evidence base is primarily laboratory and field studies.

Managerial Implications

- For aesthetic products, managers should seek to bring together consumers with similar preferences, particularly those who like, as opposed to dislike, the same alternatives. For functional products, managers should seek to facilitate consumers' access to experts.

- Managers should develop tools to help consumers accurately learn others' preferences and accurately evaluate which agents are likely to be most successful.
- Managers should encourage rapid, plentiful, interactive communication between consumers seeking and providing information.
- Managers should proceed with caution when seeking to act as advisors in order to reduce consumer skepticism and distrust.

Contributor
Andrew D. Gershoff, University of Texas at Austin

References
Gershoff, Andrew D., Ashesh Mukherjee, and Anirban Mukhopadhyay (2007), "Few Ways to Love, But Many Ways to Hate: Attribute Ambiguity, and the Positivity Effect in Agent Evaluation." *Journal of Consumer Research* 33 (4), 499–505.

Lerouge, Davy, and Luk Warlop (2006), "Why It Is So Hard to Predict Our Partner's Product Preferences: The Effect of Target Familiarity on Prediction Accuracy." *Journal of Consumer Research* 33 (December), 393–402.

Weiss, Allen M., Nicholas H. Lurie, and Deborah J. MacInnis (2008), "Listening to Strangers: Whose Responses Are Valuable, How Valuable Are They, and Why?" *Journal of Marketing Research* 45 (August), 425–36.

Vulnerable Consumers

36

Children and Advertising

Children do not respond to advertising and promotion in the same way as adults. Young children, in particular, do not have the same understanding and knowledge of advertising as older children and adults. For example, young children who are less than 7 or 8 years of age:

- Do not fully understand the persuasive intent of advertising and promotion. Young children often see advertisements as informative and entertaining without understanding that the true purpose of advertising is to persuade viewers and sell products.
- Do not fully understand the true difference between commercials and program content. Young children do not realize that programs are meant to entertain and commercials are meant to sell products, and can have difficulty separating advertising and program content when they are intermingled (e.g., commercials featuring characters from a TV program).
- Are overly trusting of advertising and promotions. Young children do not understand that advertisers exaggerate and use overly enthusiastic product claims to get across their selling points.

Evidence Base

Review of 25 years of empirical research published in major marketing and communication journals, including 21 articles supporting the three conclusions described above.

Managerial Implications

Special consideration is needed in designing advertising and promotion for young children (under 7–8 years of age) to avoid being unfair and misleading. Marketers should avoid promoting products in ways that make it more difficult for younger children to identify it as advertising—for example, using product placements in programs, movies, and online content such as games. Exaggerated product claims, superlative language (e.g., amazing, the best), and unrealistic product-use demonstrations should be avoided.

Contributor
Deborah Roedder John, University of Minnesota

Reference
John, Deborah Roedder (1999), "Consumer Socialization of Children: A Retrospective Look at Twenty-Five Years of Research." *Journal of Consumer Research* 26 (December), 183–213.

37

Aging Consumers

As consumers age, their consumption patterns shift along with such factors as goals, mental functioning, and economic resources. Seniors (typically defined as over 65 years old) generally continue to function effectively and independently in everyday life until their late 70s, unless confronted with chronic illnesses or physical limitations. Seniors experience predictable declines in working memory (capacity to retain information for short durations), speed of processing, and long-term memory. Learning new information becomes more difficult, especially when it is complex and requires effortful deliberative processing.

Expertise (or accumulated experience) can partly compensate for age-related declines in processing abilities. Older adults tend to be judicious in how they allocate their processing resources; that is, they selectively attend to information that is relevant and meaningful to them. In particular, they are motivated by goals that promote social connectedness and have emotional meaning. Older adults, compared to young adults, are more satisfied with their lives, and also report higher customer satisfaction levels for a broad range of products and services.

Evidence Base

Compilation of 25 academic papers, reporting over 100 empirical studies in marketing and psychology. Evidence is from a large number of laboratory-based and a few survey-based studies and varies by insight (ranging from 3 to 25+ studies).

Managerial Implications

Managers should account for age-related changes in goals, motivations, and processing abilities when developing products and designing communications that target older consumers. Older consumers place greater value on products and services that are emotionally meaningful; they avoid products that have complex features, especially if the products are new.

Contributor
Carolyn Yoon, University of Michigan

References
Peters, Ellen, Thomas M. Hess, Daniel Västfjäll, and Corinne Auman (2007), "Adult Age Differences in Dual Information Processes: Implications for the Role of Affective and Deliberative Processes in Older Adults' Decision Making." *Perspectives on Psychological Science* 2 (1), 1–23.

Yoon, Carolyn, Catherine A. Cole, and Michelle Lee (2009), "Consumer Decision Making and Aging: Current Knowledge and Future Directions." *Journal of Consumer Psychology* 19 (1), 2–16.

38

Effects of Low Literacy on Consumer Decision Making

Low literacy leads to difficulty with abstractions and to two related cognitive predilections: concrete thinking and pictographic thinking. *Concrete thinking* or *reasoning* involves using a single piece of information (e.g., price, ingredient, size) without regard to the product attribute it represents, and often without combining it with other pieces of information to form higher-level abstractions.

At its extreme, concrete thinking is manifest in very low levels of literacy in focusing on price (buying the cheapest), without abstracting across price and size. As a result, comparing products on multiple dimensions and making trade-offs (e.g., evaluations based on unit price) becomes more difficult with low levels of literacy. Concrete thinking also manifests in reliance on familiar brands, products, and shopping environments, and the use of numerical information without understanding the meaning (e.g., not buying products close to expiry dates as a rule of thumb but unable to explain why).

These insights on concrete thinking in the marketplace are echoed in non-marketing domains, such as in the study of low-literate peasants in Central Asia in the early 20th century. When presented with a set of objects such as hammer-saw-log-hatchet and asked to select three that formed a group or could be described with a word, they grouped the objects around concrete tasks such as chopping firewood (i.e., saw-log-hatchet), rather than the more abstract concept of tools (i.e., hammer-saw-hatchet). Thus, low literacy leads to use of concrete, visual, graphical information and a focus on how things can be used in day-to-day situations.

Pictographic thinking attaches literal and concrete meaning, rather than abstract or metaphorical meaning, to elements like colors, font, illustrations, and even words. Using pictographic thinking, consumers might keep shopping totals by visualizing currency (e.g., visualizing $5 bills and removing bills as products are purchased), decide on quantities to purchase by visualizing ingredients used during product usage (e.g., how much sugar to buy to bake a cake), and repurchase products based on viewing and remembering brand names as images.

At its extreme, pictographic thinking is manifest in very low levels of literacy in an extraordinary, and almost exclusive, focus on pictorial elements of information to draw inferences and make decisions (e.g., using actual package size and height to make price-size tradeoffs, or inferring what is in a package literally from pictures on it).

Differences in memory for brand names between low and moderately literate consumers are reduced when brand signatures with pictorial elements, rather than plain words representing brands, are used. Thus, representing brands with pictorial elements (i.e., brand signatures) leads to enhanced memory for lower literacy levels, when compared to those at higher literacy levels. This effect occurs as a result of pictorial elements that have a 1–1 correspondence with reality (e.g., actual brand signatures found in the marketplace rather than fictitious brand signatures), rather than pictorial elements per se. Similarly, low-literate consumers benefit to a greater extent from graphical nutritional labels, when compared to consumers with higher levels of literacy.

Evidence Base

In-depth interviews, observational research, and experimental studies.

Managerial Implications

Managers should seek to change their mindset and question implicit assumptions based on their own higher level of literacy. One way to do this is by conducting sustained market research on low-literate consumers.

Managers should also create a friendly shopping environment with employees trained to be sensitive to the needs of consumers with differing levels of literacy, to develop relationships, and to offer individualized assistance to consumers without embarrassing them.

Other efforts might include:
- Providing shopping cart aids that scan products, provide unit price comparisons, and maintain a running total in a low-literate user-friendly format.
- Educating consumers through concretizing information (e.g., unit price, ingredients, healthiness information).
- Organizing shelfspace thematically by usage situations.
- Presenting unit prices, sizes, prices, and discounts pictorially/graphically, rather than through percentages (e.g., dollar bills to represent price, visuals or pie charts of fractions off); presenting final prices in familiar and consistent format.

- Using pictorial store signs, and instructions, as well as familiar logos, display formats, and store layouts.

Contributor
Madhu Viswanathan, University of Illinois

References

Luria, Aleksandr R. (1976), *Cognitive Development: Its Cultural and Social Foundations*. Cambridge, Mass.: Harvard University Press.

Viswanathan, Madhubalan, Manoj Hastak, and Roland Gau (2009), "Enabling Processing of Nutritional Labels Among Low-Literate Consumers." *Journal of Public Policy and Marketing* 28 (Fall), 135–45.

Viswanathan, Madhubalan, Jose Antonio Rosa, and James Harris (2005), "Decision-Making and Coping by Functionally Illiterate Consumers and Some Implications for Marketing Management." *Journal of Marketing* 69 (1), 15–31.

Viswanathan, Madhubalan, Lan Xia, Carlos Torelli, and Roland Gau (2009), "Understanding the Influence of Literacy on Consumer Memory: The Role of Pictorial Elements." *Journal of Consumer Psychology* 19 (July), 389–402.

Health and Well-being

39

Effects of Nutrition Information and Health Claims on Consumption

Insights

Although a large proportion of consumers express interest in obtaining and using nutrition information, only a minority actively searches for and uses this information. Nutrition labels are generally poorly understood. Understanding increases when nutrition labels contain only the most important information and when they are prescriptive (e.g., with traffic lights) and comparative (e.g., with respect to daily recommended values or compared to other similar products). Graphical representations help, particularly for illiterate consumers.

Health is only the fourth or fifth most important driver of food choices. By far the largest driver is taste, and most consumers (especially men and especially in the U.S.) expect that taste is negatively associated with nutrition quality in most categories. For this reason, nutrition labels have little effect on actual food choices, except for highly involved yet less knowledgeable consumers, for unfamiliar brands, and when used to back up health claims.

Serving size information typically has no effect, and consumers use individual package size, not serving size, to represent the appropriate amount to eat. Adding calorie data to restaurant menus typically has weak or no effects but reduces consumption when the calorie count is much higher than what consumers expected, for parents ordering for their children, or for more educated consumers.

Health and nutrition claims (e.g., "low-fat," "strong heart") can strongly influence sales and consumption when they are new and unique in the category and displayed on the package front in the form of simple claims. Because consumers tend to generalize health claims and use them to categorize food as healthy or unhealthy, health claims cause consumers to underestimate calories and to increase actual (but not perceived) calorie intake once the food has been chosen (the "health halo" effect).

In addition, choosing (or just considering) a food claiming to be healthy leads people to choose more indulgent side dishes in the same meal or more indulgent food in following consumption occasions. This licensing effect occurs because health claims make people think that they can eat more without breaking their dietary goals, because they make people hungrier, and because they reduce guilt. Consumers, especially dieters, estimate that a combination of healthy and unhealthy food (e.g., a salad and burger) has fewer calories than the unhealthy food alone. This effect disappears when consumers are primed to think about food quantity (not just quality) and when they estimate calories sequentially.

Evidence Base

Dozens of consumption studies, mostly conducted in laboratory settings.

Managerial Implications

- To understand the effects of nutrition information and health claims, managers cannot rely on consumers' self-reports and should study actual behavior.
- Consumers are confused by health and nutrition information and use simple heuristics, such as categorizing food as "healthy" or "not healthy" based on simple cues.
- Nutrition quality does not have an unequivocal positive effect on consumer decisions because of negative taste inferences. Segmentation and offering multiple versions are a must, especially if health and nutrition are used as a point of difference.
- Managers need to distinguish between the effects of nutrition information and health claims on brand choice (purchase incidence, purchase quantity) and consumption (frequency and quantity).

Contributor
Pierre Chandon, INSEAD

References
Chandon, Pierre, and Brian Wansink (2011), "Is Food Marketing Making Us Fat? A Multi-Disciplinary Review." *Foundations and Trends in Marketing* 5 (3), 113–96.

Chandon, Pierre, and Brian Wansink (2007), "The Biasing Health Halos of Fast-Food Restaurant Health Claims: Lower Calorie Estimates and Higher Side-Dish Consumption Intentions." *Journal of Consumer Research* 34 (3), 301–14.

Chernev, Alexander, and David Gal (2010), "Categorization Effects in Value Judgments: Averaging Bias in Evaluating Combinations of Vices and Virtues." *Journal of Marketing Research* 47 (4), 738–47.

Grunert, Klaus G., Lisa E. Bolton, and Monique M. Raats (2011), "Processing and Acting upon Nutrition Labeling on Food: The State of Knowledge and New Directions for Transformative Consumer Research." In *Transformative Consumer Research for Personal and Collective Well-Being*, eds. David Glen Mick, Simone Pettigrew, Julie L. Ozanne, and Cornelia Pechmann. New York, N.Y.: Routledge.

40

Mass-media Campaigns and Health-related Behaviors

Insights

Mass-media campaigns can produce positive changes and prevent negative changes in health-related behaviors across large populations.

Success in mass-media campaigns is strengthened when:
- Campaigns include the use of multiple interventions (e.g., additional workplace and/or school interventions).
- Health-related behaviors are one-off or episodic (e.g., screening, vaccination) rather than habitual or ongoing (e.g., food choices, sun exposure, physical activity).
- Campaigns include easy access to relevant services and products (e.g., fresh fruits and vegetables, vaccines, condoms).
- Policies back up campaign messages (e.g., seat belt enforcement, smoking bans).
- Campaigns are sustained over time.

Success in mass-media campaigns is weakened when:
- Competitive messages from society or from the marketplace are pervasive (e.g., social norms around suntanning; cigarette marketing).
- The health threat involves addiction (e.g., drug use).

Evidence Base

Searches of seven databases in public health, social sciences, and business; identified review articles from 1998 onward on each of several mass-media campaign topics. Review findings supplemented with empirical studies published after the date of the last reviews, totaling more than 500 empirical studies.

To improve their effectiveness, mass-media campaigns should be included in comprehensive approaches to improve population health behavior. Sufficient resources in mass media should be invested over time to enable frequent and widespread exposure to campaign messages, especially for ongoing behaviors (e.g., physical activity). Promoted services and products (e.g., condoms, immunization sites) should be readily available to the target audience. In addition, complementary policy decisions that support change (e.g., smoking bans) should be considered.

Contributors

Melanie A. Wakefield, Centre for Behavioral Research in Cancer, Cancer Council, Victoria, Barbara Loken, University of Minnesota, and Robert C. Hornik, University of Pennsylvania

References

Davis, Ronald M., Elizabeth A. Gilpin, Barbara Loken, K. Vish Viswanath, and Melanie A. Wakefield (eds.) (2008), "The Role of the Media in Promoting and Reducing Tobacco Use," National Cancer Institute, Tobacco Control Monograph No. 19, NIH Publication Number 07-6242. Bethesda, Md.: U.S. Department of Health and Human Services, National Institutes of Health, National Cancer Institute.

Hornik, Robert C. (ed.) (2002), *Public Health Communication*. Mahwah, N.J.: Lawrence Erlbaum Associates.

Wakefield, Melanie A., Barbara Loken, and Robert C. Hornik (2010), "Use of Mass-Media Campaigns to Change Health Behaviour." *The Lancet* 376 (9748), 1261–71.

41

Perceptions of Health Risks

Insights

How people perceive their risk for various diseases often influences their decisions and behaviors related to health. Marketers and public policy advocates frequently try to shape perceptions of risk in a way that encourages consumers to comply with desired and cautious behaviors, whether it is using a sunscreen, eating healthy, or getting tested for hepatitis or depression. Several factors determine consumers' acceptance of their vulnerability and openness to risk information and, consequently, how effectively risk perceptions translate to behavior. These can be classified as motivational (drivers of behavior), affective (feelings), and cognitive (thoughts).

Motivational factors

Consumers want to live healthy lives. This desire may motivate them to follow healthier lifestyles, but may also cause them to believe that they are less at risk than people around them. Assuming they are invulnerable makes consumers less likely to attend to health messages and follow healthier lifestyles.

Affective factors

Entertaining the thought that one is at risk for a disease or is vulnerable to a health hazard is unpleasant; such thoughts also represent uncertainty. Consumers tend to steer clear of such unpleasantness and uncertainty.

Cognitive factors

Consumers rely on information from memory to judge their risk (e.g., how often I have unprotected sex as a risk factor for hepatitis). Ease and accuracy of recall affects consumer judgment of risk.

Salient reference points embedded in messages influence risk perceptions (e.g., framing in terms of "you are at risk" versus the "an average American is at risk" or "every day" versus "every year"). Personal, vivid, and proximal reference points are most effective in influencing consumer compliance.

Consumers are more likely to comply with a message when they believe that the solutions provided will work and can be easily implemented.

Evidence Base

Sixty studies across 28 papers across several domains and contexts, primarily laboratory based.

Managerial Implications

- Overcoming consumer optimism is critical to enhancing persuasiveness of messages.
- Health messages should strategically choose to include risk factors that make the risk seem tangible, personal, and proximal.
- Health messages should communicate risk information in a setting that does not make consumers defensive (e.g., by fostering a positive emotional environment or tone).
- Health messages can increase compliance by emphasizing that the risk-reducing behaviors advocated in the message are effective at reducing/managing the risk and can be easily implemented.
- To effectively communicate information about health risk, messages need to make it easier for the audience to cope with such negativity and uncertainty. This includes presenting the information in environments that foster positive feelings (e.g., positive versus negative framing of messages).
- Health messages that use tactics that enable easy recall of such information will influence risk perceptions. Such tactics include type of risk factor presented, vividness of risk, and its consequences.

Contributors
Nidhi Agrawal, Northwestern University, and Geeta Menon, New York University

References
Keller, Anand P., and Donald R. Lehmann (2008), "Designing Effective Health Communications: A Meta-Analysis." *Journal of Public Policy and Marketing* 27 (2), 117–30.

Luce, Mary Frances (2005), "Decision Making as Coping." *Health Psychology* 24 (4), S23–S28.

Menon, Geeta, Priya Raghubir, and Nidhi Agrawal (2008), "Health Risk Perceptions and Consumer Psychology." In *The Handbook of Consumer Psychology*, eds. Curtis P. Haugtvedt, Paul M. Herr, and Frank R. Kardes, 981–1010. New York, N.Y.: Lawrence Erlbaum and Associates.

42

Effects of Portion/ Package Size and Shape on Consumption

Insights

Larger portion sizes increase food consumption and are not compensated by lower consumption in future meals. Consumption increases of 30% are reported frequently, even for foods with low palatability and even when the calorie count of the food is also increased (i.e., volume drives consumption, not actual calorie content). Virtual size change (e.g., larger serving size cues for the same quantity) can also increase consumption, as does "labeling down" size branding (renaming a "large" a "medium"). Increasing the size of serving utensils, plates, and particularly bowls or glasses, also increases consumption. The exceptions are children under three and very small sizes that "fly below the radar" and are perceived to be healthy (but only in the short term, for restrained eaters, or when self-regulation has been activated).

There are several explanations for these effects, including social norms ("clean up your plate") and inferences about appropriate serving sizes (e.g., thinking that one is supposed to eat the entire content of the package). However, these explanations cannot explain why size increases lead to overeating even when the small size is too large to be eaten entirely and why consumers are unaware of these effects.

For these reasons, and because consumers eyeball portion and package sizes for their own consumption rather than checking size information, the most common explanation is that consumers are influenced by the following perceptual biases:

1 Size perceptions (and thus preferences) are context dependent. People avoid extreme sizes and imitate the choices of others, particularly if these other people are not obese.
2 Elongated packages appear bigger. As a result, people pour less volume into (and drink less from) a tall, thin glass than into an equi-volume short, fat glass.
3 Perceptions of size changes are inelastic: a 100% increase in size looks like a 50%–70% increase. As a result, small portions tend to be accurately estimated but large portions are greatly underestimated. These biases are the same regardless of the individual's body mass index or nutrition involvement and do not disappear through training or motivation.
4 The lack of sensitivity to increasing sizes is even stronger when packages and portions increase in all three dimensions (height, width, and length) compared to when they

only increase in one dimension. This happens because people fail to adequately compound the changes of multiple dimensions.

Evidence Base

Dozens of consumption studies, in the field and in the laboratory, for durations of up to two weeks. Studies of size perceptions and preferences are mostly laboratory based and include magnitude estimation tasks, magnitude production tasks, and choice tasks.

Managerial Implications

- Managers should actively manage and brand their package and portion sizes, not just the price or quality of their products.
- If the goal is to increase usage, managers should supersize in one dimension but downsize using all three dimensions. They should also remove the smallest size and add a larger size to the portfolio of sizes.
- If the goal is to decrease usage, managers should elongate their packages. This reduces the perceived size loss compared to proportional downsizing and, even more, compared to reducing only one dimension of the package.
- Consumers pay less attention and are less sensitive to size changes than to other changes in the marketing mix, and therefore feel cheated when stealth downsizing changes are exposed.
- Managers can overcome consumers' perceptual biases by making the size increases more visible, thereby reducing consumer demand for quantity discounts.

Contributor
Pierre Chandon, INSEAD

References
Chandon, Pierre, and Brian Wansink (2011), "Is Food Marketing Making Us Fat? A Multi-Disciplinary Review." *Foundations and Trends in Marketing* 5 (3), 113–96.

Chandon, Pierre, and Nailya Ordabayeva (2009), "Supersize in One Dimension, Downsize in Three Dimensions: Effects of Spatial Dimensionality on Size Perceptions and Preferences." *Journal of Marketing Research* 46 (6), 739–53.

Rolls, Barbara J., Liane S. Roe, and Jennifer S. Meengs (2007), "The Effect of Large Portion Sizes on Energy Intake Is Sustained for 11 Days." *Obesity* 15 (6), 1535–43.

Steenhuis, Ingrid, and Willemijn Vermeer (2009), "Portion Size: Review and Framework for Interventions." *International Journal of Behavioral Nutrition and Physical Activity* 6 (1), 58–67.

Concluding Comments

The study of consumer behavior is in essence the study of human behavior as it relates to the consideration, choice, and consumption of products and services. As the field grew, the *Journal of Consumer Research* was launched in 1974 (the year I graduated from high school), and the Association for Consumer Research held its first conference in 1968. Over the years, consumer researchers—mainly at universities—have produced a large body of knowledge that potentially illuminates many important aspects of consumer behavior.

Any company in the B2C world is intensely interested in understanding its current and potential customers. Market research departments have given way to "consumer insights" and "shopper insights" departments, as companies have struggled to answer critical questions regarding their customers and facilitate the conversion of data to knowledge to actionable insights. This is truer in today's information-intensive, hyper-competitive environment than ever before.

This volume is a step toward mapping theory-based, generalizable findings to many of the important topics with which many firms are grappling. The topics addressed cover a broad range of consumer behavior–related phenomena, including process-related issues such as search, attitudes, and decision making, marketing action–related issues such as pricing, branding, packaging, and advertising, and market segments such as children, the elderly, and low-literate consumers.

The difficulty in tackling a project like this is condensing several decades of academic research on consumer behavior into a concise, digestible form. In that regard, a couple of thoughts are in order.

First, although the insights and implications are, by design, brief, their evidence bases are not. Via the list of key references, the authors intend to point interested readers to the reams of research that underlie their insight. If one of the summaries piques your interest, I urge you to take a look at these key references, or to follow up with the author.

Second, this book is not intended to be the last word on any of the issues covered herein. Instead, it is part of a continuing dialogue between universities and industry around issues of mutual interest. Business schools lag behind our counterparts in the health sciences and engineering in the area of industry-sponsored research. Such efforts are central to MSI's mission to serve as the bridge between universities and companies vis-à-vis enabling and encouraging research that yields generalizable insights. It is appropriate and proper for this volume to connect companies with marketing scholars to move our field forward.

Jeff Inman
Marketing Science Institute Academic Trustee
Albert Wesley Frey Professor of Marketing
Katz Graduate School of Business at the University of Pittsburgh

About the Editor

Joseph W. Alba is Distinguished Professor of Marketing and chair of the Department of Marketing at the University of Florida Warrington College of Business, where he has been a faculty member since 1981. His research focuses on decision making, brand equity, product design, and pricing. He is a recipient of the Marketing Science Institute H. Paul Root Award, the American Marketing Association Louis Stern Award, and the Sheth Foundation / *Journal of Consumer Research* Award. In addition, he has twice been the recipient of the *Journal of Consumer Research* Best Article Award, and has twice been a finalist for the *Journal of Marketing Research* William F. O'Dell Award.

Alba is a Fellow of the Society for Consumer Psychology, the American Psychological Association, and the Association for Consumer Research. He has received the Distinguished Scientific Contribution Award from the Society for Consumer Psychology and the Paul D. Converse Award from the American Marketing Association and was named a Research Foundation Professor by the University of Florida. He is a past President of the Association of Consumer Research and a former associate editor of the *Journal of Consumer Research*. He has served on the editorial boards of the *Journal of Marketing Research, Journal of Marketing, Journal of Consumer Research, Journal of Consumer Psychology, International Journal of Research in Marketing, Journal of Behavioral Decision Making, Journal of Retailing,* and *Marketing Letters.* He has received "Outstanding Reviewer" awards from the *Journal of Marketing, Journal of Consumer Psychology,* and twice from the *Journal of Consumer Research.*

His teaching focuses on marketing strategy and new product development in the University of Florida MBA and executive MBA programs. He is the recipient of more than a dozen MBA "Outstanding Teacher" awards, and his Ph.D. students have won several Robert Ferber *Journal of Consumer Research* dissertation awards and John Howard AMA Dissertation Awards.